Praise for *Dance of the Archetypes*

Whether or not you consider yourself an astrologer, this book will surprise you. Diana Badger reveals the zodiac as a living set of archetypes—mirrored in the seasons, in the land beneath our feet, and in the unfolding of our inner lives. Her writing is grounded, poetic, and deeply human. *Dance of the Archetypes* invites us into a felt sense of connection with the Earth at a time when such connection is urgently needed.

Badger's work stands in beautiful conversation with contemporary thinkers exploring consciousness, interconnection, and the more-than-human world. Each chapter follows an archetype as it breathes through nature, psychology, and culture—bringing astrology into vibrant relationship with ecology, myth, and everyday life.

With her understanding of both stars and soil, Diana Badger invites us into a deeper listening—one that honors our bodies, our places, and the vast cosmic patterns that hold us. A wise and wonderfully accessible book.

~ Rhonda Fabian, editor, *Kosmos Journal*

In this delightful book, Diana skillfully guides us in exploring the magic of the signs of the zodiac. Structured as 12 essays that you can dip into for inspiration, taken as a whole, *Dance of the Archetypes* weaves a coherent narrative tapestry about the psychological and spiritual essence of astrology.

Each chapter brings the author's wisdom, photography, and voluminous study to bear upon the astrological archetypes, bringing joy to the contemplation of a subject dear to my heart. It's hard to imagine anyone reading this book not finding a fresh inspiration about astrology and the life it so richly symbolises!

~ Mark Jones, astrologer, author of *Healing the Soul* and *The Soul Speaks*

The range of ideas, images and stories in this book allow us to be more like initiates than visitors in the intricate realms of astrology. In helping identify archetypal themes and recurring patterns in our lives, *Dance of the Archetypes* enacts the ancient practice of bringing heavenly wisdom down to earth.

~ Michael Meade, author of *Awakening the Soul* and *Fate and Destiny*

Dance of the Archetypes is a luminous act of remembering and relevance. Diana Badger brings to life an ancient system of meaning-making and, through vibrant color, thought, and beauty, weaves it back into the fabric of everyday life. In this way, she restores astrology to its rightful place as a living dialogue between earth and sky, body and cosmos.

Diana's voice is a true tapestry—rich with scholarship, seasoned by experience, and offered with a mellifluous clarity that feels both grounded and expansive. It is heard not only in her words, but also through her photography: meditations drawn from the natural world that mirror and deepen the text. Diana guides the reader into conversation with the great scholars and cosmologies that shaped this work, while keeping the writing clear and welcoming—making the book both a primer and a work of depth.

Dance of the Archetypes is a wise and benevolent companion to carry through the year, as months turn and archetypes shift—inviting us to expect and trust the waves of change that shape our lives. This book is a gift for anyone longing to reunite earth and heaven, time and eternity, as a lived relationship.

~ Anne Wiesen, Ed.M, MS, Herbalist, Educator, and Co-Founder of *Design by Plants*

Dance of the Archetypes offers a personal perspective on the meaning of the zodiac signs and how the archetypes manifest in our day-to-day life. It encourages reflection on our own experience and reveals new perspectives and surprising connections that enrich your understanding of how astrology works. The book is illustrated with beautiful and intriguing images that inspire insights and new ways of seeing that add another dimension to our perception.

The text emphasises the importance of bringing the abstract language of astrology down to earth and understanding it through everyday experiences. The stars aren't just up there in the heavens. They are also down here within the imagination and synchronicities of daily life. Astrology is alive and speaks to us through the interconnected web of life, becoming part of our 'lived experience.'

I loved the photographs and paintings and enjoyed the well-chosen quotes scattered through the text. These encouraged me to pause and contemplate the deeper meaning of the signs in my own life and I ended up with a long list of books to read! *Dance of the Archetypes* provides an excellent introduction to how the adage 'as above, so below' actually works in astrology and I highly recommend the book.

~ Jessica Davidson, astrologer, writer

From the opening words of *Dance of the Archetypes*, we are drawn into a magical place—not only between Earth and Sky, but also between poetry and prose, past and present, our individual journey and our shared consciousness. With an open and inviting voice, Diana welcomes us into her work, no matter where we are in our astrological pursuits, allowing astrology to "roam free in the wilds of ordinary life."

As a true "gatherer of esoteric wisdom," Diana weaves together astrology, depth psychology, mythology, alchemy, the imaginal realms, and great beauty: page after page, we are guided through her luminous photographs of flowers and rocks, earth and sky. Diana's perceptive eye is as expansive as it is deep, filling her pages with color and awe.

The magic and mystery of life come alive here, held within a container of persistent hope. Take your time with this book—there is much to absorb, and Diana has so much to share.

~ Sherrie Lovler, artist, author of *On Softer Ground: Paintings, Poems and Calligraphy*

Diana Badger's *Dance of the Archetypes* brings astrology, ecology, and depth psychology into a coherent vision of a living cosmos. She traces the interconnections between planetary movements, the intelligence of the Earth, and the symbolic life of the human psyche, allowing meaning to emerge through attentiveness to patterns and resonance, rather than abstraction.

Badger writes with confidence across astrological practice, an embodied relationship with Nature, and archetypal imagination. The book is enriched by her photographs which function not merely as illustrations but as parallel modes of knowing. Her images invite a contemplative engagement that extends beyond language, deepening the book's psychological and ecological themes. Readers entering this terrain will find themselves guided by a voice that is not only knowledgeable, but also embraces mystery.

~ Jon. G. Jackson, M.D., neuroscientist and poet

As a psychotherapist, I deeply appreciate Diana Badger's *Dance of the Archetypes* for its skillful and creative integration of the astrological archetypes with psychological and earth-based wisdom. She presents complex ideas in a user-friendly way that lends itself to grounded personal insights and growth for the reader. Her writing is a joy to read as it flows forth from the deep well of her knowledge and intuition.

~ Tina Stanley, LCSW

Dance of the Archetypes delivers valuable astrological wisdom in an engaging style that is easily accessible to the lay audience. With a depth and breadth gained from decades of outer as well as inner studies, Badger deftly weaves together concepts of astrology, psychology, earth wisdom, and contemporary world events. In so doing, she has created a work in which readers can easily locate themselves, and reach new insights. Most importantly, the book explores the fundamental archetypal signatures and guidance inherent in astrology, which if applied, serve to both enhance consciousness development and achieve practical, material plane fulfillment.

~ Rio Olesky, astrologer, author of *Astrology & Consciousness*
and *Manual For the Modern Mystic*

DANCE OF THE ARCHETYPES

How Astrology Informs Our Lives and Connects Us to the Earth

Diana Badger

ELEMENTAL BOOKS
San Francisco, California

Published by Elemental Books
elementalbks@gmail.com

ISBN 979-8-9943550-0-8 (paperback)
ISBN 979-8-9943550-1-5 (ebook)

LCCN: 2026900224

Cover photo and all interior photos by Diana Badger
Book Design: Clarity Designworks

✧

Welcome to the realm of Earth and Sky—
of all things interconnected:
of the wisdom and beauty of the stars & planets,
the blessed Earth, and we betwixt,
weaving our way between
our own journeys and our communities.

✧

CONTENTS

Introduction

Are not flowers the stars of the earth?
~ Clara Lucas Balfour[1]

What's in a star? What's in a flower? Ultimately, along with Mystery, the star, the flower, and we ourselves are one and the same, woven of the unitive fabric of life, teeming with shared minerals, and consciousness.

With this in mind, it is my intent to share with you my particular lens of perception, one that sees our human lives through both astrology and earth connectedness, weaving them together to help us better understand our place within the matrix of Earth and Sky.

From the point of view of the stars, what you have before you is the distillation of my gleanings and playful observations of how the 12 zodiacal signs—which I consider as archetypes—reflect their signatures in our lives. These were initially shared in my *Earth Sky Journal* writings as the Sun passed through each sign, and I have now compiled, sifted, and combed them through for more studied perusal. I also include my ruminations on the slower moving, but impactful outer (transpersonal) planets within the current longer cycle of years, from 2026 on up through 2043, when the slowest planet, Pluto leaves Aquarius. These outer planets impact culture as a whole, and taking cues from them helps us move in step with the cosmos.

I write from the premise that the movements of the celestial bodies offer messages and meaning for us regardless of what our particular natal chart configuration may be. We all walk the earth in sync with the beams of the Sun, the Moon, and the planets of our solar system, whether we know it or not.

My ambition with this book is that it offer something for all, regardless of where you are on the spectrum of astrological knowledge. You will see that I draw correspondences between the archetypes and the earth's seasonal cycles as well as a broad range of wisdom teachings, cultural references, and our psychological lives. This should be of interest to new as well as long-term students and practitioners of astrology. My aim is to release astrology from its confines in the realms of abstract thought, so that it can start to roam free in the 'wilds' of ordinary life, and thereby reveal the mystery of Oneness that is ever afoot.

This book is also intended for lovers of the earth interested to learn how the manifestations of the Divine in the natural world interrelate with the signatures of the stars. And, it is for those interested to peruse my photographs sprinkled through these pages. I know I do have some 'readers' who like to absorb my images as much as they do my text! All good!

✧

From the point of view of the flowers—as well as the trees, the birds, the waters, and much more—my mission is to highlight the profound interconnectedness of Earth and Sky, and to turn our attention earthwards, away from the purely mental abstractions through which astrology so easily captivates. As a Virgo Sun sign, I am a perfect illustration of the blending of 'above and below.' Virgo is an Earth sign, intrinsically connected to the earth and its domain, and yet ruled by Mercury, an Airy planet, that informs communication, learning, and analysis.

Thereby, archetypal Virgo—like many interested in astrology—does love to spend time in her head! But we are in a time when it is ever more crucial that we move down from our heads and into our bodies, into the body of the Earth, and into our hearts. So you will find the themes of earth connection, body connection, and love of the earth woven throughout these pages.

The planet Mercury is named after the Roman god Mercury—counterpart to Greek god Hermes—and associated with Hermes Trismegistus, who was renowned in antiquity for his teachings of Hermeticism, which include alchemy, magic, and astrology. Accordingly, while I am not an academic scholar, I am a gatherer of esoteric wisdom, and there will be smatterings of references to such topics in the pages ahead.

Hermes Trismegistus was known for coining the seminal phrase, *As above, so below.* And it is my intent to share with you glimpses of how this Truth has visited me over the 2.5 years that I have offered myself to weaving the loom of Earth and Sky.

Origins

I have been a lover of many aspects of the natural world throughout my life, and have used photography to capture its magic since I received my first Kodak Brownie camera at age 11. At around this same age, I began my explorations of astrology, having discovered with my best friend the little Dell books on the topic on a spinning rack at the drugstore.

A turning point came at age 18, when my older brother gave me my first official astrology book, *Astrological Psychology*, by Karen Hamaker-Zondag. Marking my first encounter with Carl G. Jung's ideas about the psychological depths, it was love at first read, and has been my angle on astrology ever since—that of using this magnificent lens on "reality" to deepen and broaden our understanding of ourselves, those we relate with, and the ever-changing world around us, so that we may heal, and transform according to our highest potential.[2]

I began writing my *Earth Sky Journal* blog in early 2023. I wasn't sure of the specifics at the outset, but I knew I wanted to weave together and make connections between these two great passions, astrology and earth connection.

Having studied and worked as a textile designer in my late 20s (over three decades ago), I had long been interested in patterns. As a designer, I found existing 'motifs' in books featuring different cultural arts through history, and replicated and arranged them into my own unique designs. Typically, the motifs reflected aspects of the natural world, which is rich with pattern. My teacher assured us that it was okay to 'copy' these old motifs, as there was 'nothing new under the Sun,' and that we were making original art simply by presenting them in our own unique designs.

I realize now that my blog posts have evolved through turning my eye for physical pattern to the mind's eye of identifying astrological patterns, seeing how they fit into our lives, and the cycles of the earth, and turning them into 'artful' designs conveying meaning. With my writings, I take existing motifs—archetypes, which live in the bedrock of the unconscious, and explore the patterns they make in interaction with each other, with the cycles of the earth, within human culture, and of course within our own psychological and spiritual lives. So while my themes are not new, the way I spin them is unique, and, one hopes, revelatory!

Sunrise over Callanish Stones, Isle of Lewis, Outer Hebrides, Scotland

Archetypes

The archetypes are considered to be the content of the collective unconscious. C.G. Jung, progenitor of depth psychology, determined that they are the building blocks of the psyche, shaping both matter and mind. Jungian analyst and author, Murray Stein, further suggests that archetypes are the building blocks of Being, and as such underlie the Self.[3] Psychological astrologer Glenn Perry suggests that the psyche is charged with archetypal energies that are at once imminent and transcendent, psychological and cosmological.[4]

The term archetype dates back to the 16th century, and has been defined as a foundational pattern of behavior, which in itself doesn't change, but which goes on to replicate in new ways, while retaining its primary signature. Examples of archetypes include the hero, the caregiver, the orphan, the rebel, the lover, and the sage. While these can exist in themselves, they can also be mapped into the astrological wheel of signs, which is the intent of archetypal astrology. By locating and recognizing archetypal themes within ourselves, we gain clarity and understanding as to our motivations, the people and events we magnetize in our lives, and the recurring patterns and cycles we experience.

Each of the 12 archetypes rules one or two of the 12 astrological 'houses' (sectors of the zodiacal wheel) in our chart, even if we have no planets in a sign. So given that we all have every sign embedded somewhere in our charts, we can find guidance, self-knowledge, and growth in considering each of them.

The archetypes are grouped according to the four elements. These inform our access to groundedness (Earth signs), passion (Fire signs), intuitive knowing (Water signs), and conceptualization (Air signs). Like the elements, each sign has things to teach us—perhaps through pointing to areas of blockage or potential that, if addressed, could open new doors, and reveal to us our giftedness or genius. With the aid of understanding both the archetypal signatures and astrology's timings—based on planetary cycles—our intimations about ourselves and our capacities are strengthened. We become emboldened to lean into our gifts at the right time, manifesting them in service to life in our unique way.

[My *Astrology Primer* section at the back will help you distinguish between planets, signs, and houses, all of which convey the archetypal energies, as well as other astrology basics.]

Calling in the Muse

Each of us looks on life through a certain perspective. The Indigenous peoples of North America teach that every point on the Medicine Wheel has its own outlook, and that as a community we benefit from sharing and learning each other's, to achieve wholeness. I would add that the perspective we choose tends to reflect either a conditioned mindset, or an updated, conscious intention through which we call in the reality we meet.

Reflecting on these few years of my Earth-Sky writings, I feel that my undertaking of intentionally calling in the astrological archetypes became, in effect, my opening myself as muse to these forces. I chose a perspective that was 'hospitable' to receiving and knowing them, and they have joined me. Outer events, numerous synchronicities in my inbox, and other 'on time' emanations have consistently come my way to help me contemplate and illustrate how the astrological themes present in the zodiacal dance show up in synchrony in our earthly lives.

Another aspect of the perspective adopted during these years since the pandemic arrived, in which we have faced a world replete with suspensions, losses, grief, and struggle on many fronts, is one of persistent hope. This includes a determination to engage with healing, creativity, and beauty, whether this be relationally in community, or in my individual pursuits. I choose optimism, but not via spiritual bypass (i.e., using lofty ideas to escape facing difficult issues.)

From a depth psychological perspective, healing, for which I consider astrology a valuable tool, requires facing what lies in the darkness within, and looking at long-repressed traumas that arise when the time ripens (typically indicated by major outer planet transits). In this way we gain both understanding and ultimately a degree of separation from our

triggers and our pain. From here, we have the opportunity to access the inner freedom needed to sing our true song.

I look on these critical and difficult times with a willingness to continue to face what's hard, trusting that this duress is given from Creator for reasons unknown, taking care not to let fear or despair drag me down or preoccupy my thinking. I have in recent years had my own intense encounters with fear (and my fair share of losses), but thanks to the grace of the powerful tools of astrology, and *The Gene Keys*,[5] as well as my decades-long Sufi practice—all of which fortify me with wisdom, patience, and self-compassion—I have faced my own inner fires and come through with the capacity to humbly offer my gifts.

Weaving of Heaven and Earth

A constant bass note throughout this book is the theme of how the 'Heavens' and the Earth are of a single piece, and how we dance with and partake of the beauty and guidance of this interconnected field.

This theme has been with us since antiquity. In his book, *Gardening as a Sacred Art*, Jeremy Naydler traces how Heaven and Earth have been united in the form of the sacred garden since earliest recorded Western history.

> *In Mesopotamia the ziggurats, which were terraced pyramids surmounted by a shrine, served the religious purpose of linking earth and heaven. They were planted with trees, shrubs and vines from at least the second millennium BC and were probably the original prototype of the legendary 'hanging gardens' of Babylon.*
>
> *[...] The temple garden, certainly in ancient Egypt and most probably also in ancient Mesopotamia, is best understood as an evocation of a mythic condition in which humans and gods lived in harmony together in a natural world that was instilled with spiritual power and meaning.*[6]

Western Astrology (aka Tropical Astrology) likewise traces its origins to Ancient Babylon where, according to Glenn Perry, heavenly powers—or the planetary gods—were considered to determine events on earth *not* through cause and effect, but because of the prevailing view that all parts of the cosmos are an interdependent, living whole. But astrological events in that time, unlike ours, were considered to be a matter of fate, whereby humans had no say in the matter other than through prayer and supplication to the gods. From the perspective of modern astrology, however, we consider that a person has free will as to how their astrological indicators manifest. No astrology chart indicates a predestined fate. Perry writes:

> *Postmodern astrology largely draws on Jung's theory of synchronicity, which postulates that archetypes not only inform and animate human consciousness, they also manifest through specific experiences that reflect the structure and dynamics of the individual psyche. Inner states and outer events are meaningfully related by an acausal connecting principle.*[7]

Alchemy

One explanation for the acausal interconnection between the planets and life on earth comes through alchemy, the ancient practice of turning base metals to gold, equated with the quest for 'the philosopher's stone.' C.G. Jung was a serious student of both alchemy and astrology, although this was not widely known, as he needed to maintain his professional profile. (Alas, astrology has through modern times been looked at with great skepticism. This I hope to do my small part in rectifying!)

Jung considered alchemy to be the 'younger sibling' of astrology, and studied and worked with both as tools for psychological transformation. In his schema, planets were seen as spheres of awareness connecting us to aspects of psychological experience. He quoted alchemists who suggested that the planets' metal constituents are spun into the earth, guiding and instructing us in our lives through their spirit-based essences. Alchemists said that the Sun, for instance, spins its gold essence into the earth.

> *The sun is the image of God, the heart is the sun's image in man, just as gold is the sun's image in the earth (also called Deus terrenus) and God is known in the Gold.*[8]

My understanding of this is that God, therefore, is known in the earth, which I hope to illustrate throughout these pages. As well as the powerful healing potential of connecting to both the natural world and its rhythms, and that of the wisdom of the planetary archetypes.

Imagination—the Great Connector

The inherent interconnection of Heaven and Earth is a strong theme as well in the Celtic tradition, reflected by respected Celtic wisdom teachers and writers, John O'Donohue and John Philip Newell. In his book, *Sacred Earth, Sacred Soul,* Newell shares the words of his spiritual forebear John Alexander Scott:

> *'The sum of the whole matter is this,' [Scott] said, that the most important work for us to do 'from year to year, from month to month, from hour to hour is to combine earth and heaven, time and eternity.' This is the role of the sacred imagination, to help us remember the 'curve of oneness' from which we have come. It will strengthen us in the sacred work of seeking true relationship with one another and the earth.*[9]

Employing the imagination to join the threads that reveal this 'true relationship' is something I engage in throughout the book, not just between the cycles of Earth and Sky, but as well with the words and ideas of the many writers and teachers I encounter in my ongoing dance with 'higher ideas'.

Depth astrology and archetypal astrology employ myth, symbol, and 'the imaginal realms' to penetrate the unseen depths. These include dreams (which I work with in my counseling practice, and have studied and done groupwork with for decades), and forms of focused day-dreaming (such as Jung's *Active Imagination*). The imaginal provides access to the layers of reality that are not visible, or knowable by the mind, but which nevertheless inform our experience. Astrology and forms of dreaming are vital tools for accessing what lies 'behind the veil' of so-called reality.

With this intent, of including other ways of seeing beyond the written word, I have interspersed my writings with my photographs, using them as playful 'helpers' to convey my ideas with more dimension, and to give the mind a 'breather'! Images of any sort speak to the unconscious, and the heart, and are vital for our fuller understanding, and delight in, the magic and mystery of life.

How to Use This Book

Dance of the Archetypes will help you get to know the flavors and whisperings of the archetypes as they dance through our world, in various ways. I encourage you to read the book straight through, to absorb the magic and wonder of all my musings on the archetypes. But you might also read chapters selectively, as celestial movements indicate—such as when the Sun passes through a sign (which is how I wrote these chapters), or the Moon, or any other transiting planet that has prominence in your chart.

I do not support 'Sun sign astrology' (although Linda Goodman's hit book on the topic in the late 60's was fun!), as this is but one aspect of astrology's complex system. However, reading the chapters about your own (or loved ones') Sun, Moon, and Rising signs could be a meaningful way to explore the archetypal flavors personal to you, as typically you will recognize these signatures. Also interesting to read would be the signs of the Lunar Nodes, which indicate where you come from—and have gained 'expertise' (South Node); and where you're headed, often an energy less familiar, but charged with calling (North Node)! (You can get a free chart cast on Astro.com.)

However you choose to use this book, I sincerely hope that you find both inspiration and delight in the chronicles of my reflections on the archetypes, and that these in some way open your capacity to listen to and move in step with them yourself. And may you come to more deeply understand and reconnect with the wisdom and healing potential of these archetypal signatures as they penetrate our Being, and learn to witness with love and awe how deeply intertwined they—and we—are with the beauty and intelligence of the blessed Earth.

SEIZE THE DAY: ARIES
~ March 21-April 19

Daffodils trumpet spring's arrival

Greetings from the moist, bursting turmoil of spring, and the Aries pulse, which invites us to gather our inner fires and meet life with a pioneering spirit and sense of mission. For Aries marks the birth of a new ecological and zodiacal year, heralded by the spring equinox, and is very much a sign of new beginnings.

Shambhala warriors

As the first sign in the zodiac, Aries is 'the child of the Universe,' ever eager to 'spring' into action. What kind of action is the important question, given that Aries, ruled by Mars, is known for its impulsivity and hot-headedness.

In its highest manifestation, Aries serves as the sacred warrior, acting courageously to protect the Cosmic Order. Speaking to this theme, beloved eco-philosopher, teacher, activist, and author Joanna Macy pointed us to the "Shambhala Warrior Prophecy" from 12 centuries ago. In a YouTube video she shares of having been told by a Tibetan master that the Shambhala Warriors are *boddhisatvas* (awakened beings who choose to return to Earth after death in order to serve humanity) who act from a boundless heart, and, importantly, that each of us has the capacity to achieve this.

The prophecy teaches that there comes a time of great danger, when the life of all beings seems to hang by a tenuous thread, being threatened by "barbarian powers" that have arisen. And that, while they waste their wealth to destroy each other, these powers have much in common, such as greed, and weapons and technologies of massive destruction.

It is told that ours is the time of the coming of the Kingdom of Shambhala, which is not a place, but something that lives in the hearts and minds of its peaceful warriors, who have neither their own terrain, nor special uniforms. The warriors of this kingdom are called to find within themselves great courage—both moral and physical—as they must go into the barbarians' fold—the corridors of power—and dismantle their weapons.

Aries' totems, the rugged ram, pose for a family shot in the Scottish Highlands

Key to this undertaking is the trust that this dismantling *can be done*, because the barbarians' weapons are *mano-maya*, meaning made by the human mind and, thereby, capable of being undone by the mind. In her retelling, Joanna stresses that the problems of today are not from evil 'out there,' but from our own ways of understanding and seeing our world—from our habits of mind. *And from our fears, and our fear of facing our fears.* Learning to see and dismantle our conditioned assumptions and perceptions is key to this warrior work, and it takes great courage, as it requires breaking with, and healing from the familiar strategies that have covered our wounds due to traumatic memory.

She goes on to share that the warriors train in the use of two primary weapons: compassion (based in the Pisces/Neptune archetype)—whose warmth is the fuel of action, and which requires being unafraid of the suffering of the world—and wisdom, or insight into the radical interdependence of the vast web of life (partaking of the Aquarius/Uranus archetype). If we're not afraid of witnessing the suffering, we can then transmute it into other conditions. These two tools, the heat of compassion and the cool insight into existence, bring balance to each other. The uncertainty of how it will turn out keeps us alive and alert, Joanna points out, and fierce courage is needed in the endeavor.

Joanna was renowned as a pioneering way shower in the area of embracing our grief over the ailing planet back in the 1980s (when I first attended one of her workshops in Berkeley, CA), and for instigating a global "Work That Reconnects" community[10] as a way to remedy our dislocation from nature and from each other. It makes good astrological sense that her natal Uranus (the Awakener archetype) was in Aries, along with her Venus (how we share our love)—and that her Venus trined (was in harmonious partnership with) Neptune, the significator of compassion and faith. In true Aries fashion, Joanna was a pioneer for a shift in consciousness.

Passion play

Given its penchant for the new, and for beginnings, the wonder-filled fire sign Aries presides over the newborn child with all her innocence and freedom of self-expression. To embrace this ethos of exploration and instinct, we might spend some time reconnecting with our own child self, with its spirit of delight and innovation. What helps us drop into the space of non-judgmental, clear-headed daring? This will be of great assistance to the rebirthing work we have before us, no matter our age, as we need to liberate the unselfconscious, intuitive spark of our being from worn-out constraints at this time of great change.

As the first Fire sign, unimpeded Aries is bursting with life. It relishes in physicality, and using its body to burn its abundance of fuel. Aries is also highly playful. Given its association with Ares, Greek god of war, this sign can be drawn to forms of rugged, or combat, play. My Aries Moon daughter loved to wrestle with her Aries Sun dad in our living room when she was young. He loved it too! He had three other planets in Aries, including Jupiter, which expands whatever it touches—in this case his Sun! And with this strong Aries signature he became a decades-long, passionate devotee of the martial art form, Aikido, including becoming a teacher to our daughter and her Aries-informed peers!

Developed by the Japanese master, Morihei Ueshiba, Aikido is a martial art characterized as "the way of unifying with life energy." Aikido's philosophy is based in learning to overcome one's disharmonious instincts that might prompt violence or aggression. In this sense, Ueshiba advocated "victory over oneself."

*Daughter Aries Moon throws
Father Aries Sun to the mat at the dojo*

I spent a fair amount of time myself (as witness only—I, with no Aries planets or points) at the Aikido dojo during the child-rearing years, given how central the practice was to both my husband and my daughter. But these days, now an empty nester, with my ex-husband on the other side, the bird life around my garden has become my family, and my entertainment!

Much as I used to enjoy watching the 'rough play' of Aikido in prior years, I now find joy watching 'my' birds. The other day, I was witness to a game of boisterous tag being played between a songful mockingbird and a Steller's jay. Entranced, I watched as mockingbird chased jay in unending gyroscopic circles through the branches of a large privet tree.

The sound of four large fluttering wings tirelessly cycling through the leafing branches, accompanied by flashes of mockingbird's white under-feathers as he angled towards jay's imposing black crown served up a circus-like marvel that had me grinning ear to ear. I like to draw the connection (as I'm wont to do) that these feathered friends were embodying the child-like spiritedness of the Aries impulse—spontaneous, freedom-loving, highly energetic, and inherently riveting (like all Fire signs!).

Magnolia tree catches the playful spirit

Elemental boost

The zodiacal wheel was originally developed by the Greeks, in synchrony with the cycles of the seasonal changes on Earth. At the Sun's ingress (entrance) into Aries at the spring equinox we are poised at the beginning of both the seasonal and astrological wheel. Hence its earthly season coincides with the blessing in the Northern hemisphere of healthy green things sprouting from the ground.

As a trained herbalist I know that some of these so-called weeds are great to ingest for spring cleansing of our livers, which may have gone sluggish while subjected to more sedentary, indulgent-inclined winter habits. In the spirit of 'it's all connected,' in Chinese medicine, the liver is considered the seat of anger, so it's apt that the earth at this time produces liver tonifying herbs to help the Aries tendency to 'lose its cool,' as its red hot ruling planet, Mars, is known for.

Speaking of excess heat, a young, curly-haired checker in a smart cap at my local Community Market recently commented on a product I was buying for inflammation (which is fueled by heat in the body), saying, "Yeah, I have all kinds of chronic inflammation. But I've found the best thing is to chew on a bit of turmeric root. That, and drinking plenty of water, getting lots of sunshine, and walking with my bare feet on the ground." A bit bad for business, I pointed out, but I was pleased to hear his well-founded advice! It got me thinking, as I then proceeded on a walk along our rain-soaked Laguna wetlands, that he was prescribing that I partake of the elements: Fire (sun), Water, and Earth! (Air goes without saying if we're out of doors.) Right up my Earth-Sky alley!

Rain-soaked Laguna de Santa Rosa, Sebastopol, in spring

This young man's words helped me imbibe the nourishment of this rare sunny day between rains, and the sounds and sight of the trickling waters coursing beside the trail in newly forged creeks. Thus filled with the dance of the elements, instinct prompted me earthwards, in search of edible spring greens to further fortify. I was rewarded with bitter but bracing dandelion leaf, sweet fennel, and warming chickweed! Years ago, I learned of the practice of eating wild weeds when travelling to a new country or region, so as to help one get grounded upon arrival in a new land. Of course, even in one's own homeland eating your wild greens is a great tonifying spring practice. (Also delish are purslane and miner's lettuce.)

Taming our instincts

Being ruled by Mars, the planet of action and desire, Aries is unimpeded by practical concerns, determined to 'just do it.' The archetype signifies the fearless pioneer, who sets out for a new land, as did my ex, having grown up in Communist Russia, and landed here in Sonoma County in the early 90s after *perestroika* freed him to follow his explorer's nature, where ultimately he became a respected teacher and permaculture expert.

We lived during our first nine years together in the remote West Sonoma County mountain-hills, where—ram-like—he regularly roamed the steep hillsides surrounding first our 350-square foot, off-grid cabin beneath the redwoods beside a creek, and then, our two-story geodesic dome home, nestled amidst steeply sloped, tree-lined hills. He crafted garden beds, steps, and pathways all with rocks from his foraging, and found suitable pieces of wood to carve—his largest creation being of a 5-foot-tall owl. He had never studied masonry or carving per se, yet knew how to work with wood and rock by sheer instinct and determination—Aries being gifted with the creative fires of instinct. (He also had an engineer's mind.)

One of the key features that enabled him to tame his restless Aries energy into concrete constructions was his natal Saturn-Neptune conjunction. With Saturn as the natural ruler of Capricorn—the Earth sign most responsible for our capacity to manifest visions and intentions on the material plane—and Neptune presiding over dreams and ideals, he had the knack for taking his findings and building useful structures; and with Neptune's influence, making them beautiful, such that they embodied the spark of the Ideal, which Neptune aspires to.

This Saturn-Neptune signature is relevant to the collective culture of our present time, as the two planets are again conjunct, now in the sign of Aries, through roughly May 2027. So we are wise to adjust our sails to catch the winds of this configuration's gifts, and take heed of its potential pitfalls.

Ideal-Real fusion: Neptune-Saturn conjunction in Aries

There are many ways to unpack this signature. The basics are that Saturn calls us to patient hard work that serves to ground our intentions on the material plane, while 'far out' blue Neptune presides over the transcendent and ever-elusive stuff of dreams, which can be both unrealistic delusions, and vital seeds, emanating from the Divine Imagination.

While astrology traditionally puts more importance on the archetypal potency of *planets*—as the actors on the stage—and less on the *signs* they're in—which describe their clothes or style of being—it is noteworthy that these two archetypal thespians are, during this potent transformational era, dressed in the garb of Aries, and that they first were conjunct in 2025 very close to the 0° Aries point, and meet exactly at that point in February '26.

0° Aries is the inception point of the zodiac, so this planetary conjunction (with a conjunction marking a new beginning in the relationship between two planets) at the zodiac's ultimate 'new beginnings' point adds a fiery rallying cry to the energy. So let us consider Saturn and Neptune in fearless pioneer/warrior Aries attire as we ponder their collaborative potential.

Saturn is the creator of the enduring structures that make up our civilizations. But life—thankfully—is about more than skyscrapers and halls of power. At the other end of the spectrum, Neptune brings in the magic on a level that operates behind the veils of the ordinary. (Gemini corresponds with magic as well, but in a different manner. More on that in that sign's chapter.)

Star-like, heavenly blue centaurea emerges from its origins as a seed in Earth's mind

As a watery planet (Neptune, counterpart of the Greek god Poseidon, being ruler of the Sea), Neptune can both erode and infuse on subtle levels. In its shadowy aspect, this archetype promotes fear in the collective psyche, in the form of negative fantasies, self-doubt, and crises of faith. The challenges of keeping our inner boat afloat are real in this time.

In its higher manifestation, Neptune is vested with the power of the imagination, which is in fact what seeds reality. If we can face our fears (as mentioned, often-times ancestral in this time of accelerated trauma healing), let them course through us, and meet them with presence and self-compassion, allowing them to thus dissipate, we can better rise to the crusade at hand. Neptune can then take the helm as divine navigator, with Saturn as earth-bound work crew. With this archetypal pairing, it *very* much matters what images and dreams we cultivate, as these will affect what comes to pass. Once a vision has in some way landed within, our work is to hold it, give it plenty of space, and allow it into the world, in its own timing (Saturn presiding over time), by sharing and living it.

Bite of the dying dog

Meanwhile, Neptune's dissolving capacity will continue the work that transformation agent Pluto has started—first when in Saturn-ruled Capricorn, from 2009-2024, during which we saw the slow toppling of tired structures and systems, and now, in Aquarius until 2044. Despite current indications, Neptune teaming up with Saturn can assist Pluto in the long work of dismantling the old paradigm of patriarchy, hierarchy, and war, in preparation for a new-old alignment in which humans harken back to pre-industrial, pre-patriarchal times to live peacefully with each other while abiding by the natural laws of Earth and Sky. The calamities we're seeing, and will see for some years or even decades most likely, are the death throes of this transition.

I recall the words of a leather-clad, longhaired 'seer' I met at the sacred Callanish Stones on Scotland's Hebridean Isle of Lewis in 2022, which I'd arrived at as the pinnacle of my own type of Aries pilgrimage, a solo e-bike journey. The man described our civilizational 'dying phase', and ascertained that the horrific acting out of this end of an era, such as we continue to see in increasing extremes, could be likened to the crazed bite of a dying animal in pain, such as a dog of its master. Death comes with suffering and sometimes anguish, and loss will continue to be present as we proceed; but along with being present with grief and compassion, we are called to fearlessness.

For this, Saturn and Neptune are well positioned in Aries—known for its courage in the face of battle. Under this 'warrior/crusader' influence (Saturn in Aries until 2028, Neptune until 2039), violence and war will likely continue to compel the shadow forces, but the powers working to birth a new paradigm are rising between the cracks. These expand and strengthen when we train our gaze on them.

Claiming personal authority

Alongside all this, Saturn-Neptune in Aries holds great potential to usher in consciousness change, urging us to 'get serious' (Saturn) about hooking ourselves up to the rising frequency of the Neptunian field of higher consciousness. Saturn's 2.5-year journey in Neptune's ruler, Pisces, was in its own way about dissolving into a 'cloud of unknowing' chrysalis phase of reformulation and uncertainty, and now, with Saturn alongside Pisces' ruler Neptune, we're getting an even stronger boost of gestational juice with which to continue fortifying the chrysalis.

All being well, at some point we die to our caterpillar selves, and begin to take new form, and forms of action. Maybe even grow some wings! This takes courage (have I said that?), seasoned with the faith that in some essential part of ourselves we can let go of Saturnian fear and rigidity and take Neptune as our guide. At its highest, Neptune funds us with faith and trust in our endeavors. Importantly, in Aries style we need to claim our heart-sourced, personal authority and harness our instincts towards what we know is true and good.

Saturn's journey through Aries is significant for us personally, with Saturn being the impulse towards goal-setting, and Aries the sign of taking initiative. With Aries' penchant for improvisation, during Saturn's stay here we are called to tap into our instincts and take creative risks on behalf of our passions. Saturn's focused energy, when filtered through fiery Aries, brings the confidence, determination, and energy to make things happen.

And, as Aries pertains to claiming *selfhood*, in these next years we are called to fearlessly take charge of our own experience as we pursue our intentions and visions, and not look outside ourselves for affirmation. This is supported by the asteroid Chiron, the wounded healer, in Aries from 2018 until June 2026, encouraging the work of healing and honing our skills of centered self-assertion.

Purifying fire of radical unknowing

When under stress, however, Saturn in Aries can show up as excess control or harshness, or as a fear of taking action. But it's also possible that when Saturn—a heavy, earthy energy that works and grows slowly through linear time—is placed in a Fire sign, especially cardinal sign Aries, Saturn's natural resistance to change can get 'fired up', generating the capacity to transform. I think of the 'hot rocks' used to fuel the Native American sweat lodge ceremony, which I participated in several times in my 20s. Indeed, the fire-heated rocks brought into the low-ceilinged dome structures turned up the heat! Likewise, Saturn in Aries can help us with the work of purification, of releasing the dross of old habits to prepare for new ways of acting for change.

Teacher and author Mirabai Starr speaks about the 'purifying fire of radical unknowingness,' and through my reading, suggests how the fire element might join with the nature of Saturn, given that Saturn's cold, hard determination often invokes the conditions of loneliness, and fear of intimacy. Quoted in the *Friends of Silence* online newsletter, she invokes the fire element, when applied to Neptune's 'radical unknowingness', as the doorway to the Divine:

> *At the mystical heart of each of the Abrahamic faiths lie teachings about the transformational power of fire and the identification of the Holy One with light. In Judaism, the Shekinah—the indwelling feminine presence of God—took the form of a pillar of fire at night to lead the Israelites through the desert.*[11]

[...] May we let ourselves down into the arms of fire and allow it to melt the armor of our hearts. The excruciating fire of our loneliness and our fear of intimacy. The sweet fire of our longing for union with the Beloved. The purifying fire of radical unknowingness, which all the great mystics assure us is the beginning of knowing God.

A great teacher on my own path of Sufism, Irina Tweedie, wrote a monumental book in diary form about her time spent with her teacher in India in her 50s. As an Aries Sun sign, she titled it, *Daughter of Fire*, pointing to how every aspect of the ego must be burned away on the spiritual path to awakening. Spiritual teacher Gangaji underscores this point, as well the Aries supreme virtue of freedom, stating, "Freedom is a necessary raging fire needed to uncover or dismantle our strategies of being. On the spiritual path, we need this fire," which she adds can get suppressed when mixed with memories that hold threads of trauma.[12] This is why healing work is so crucial for the spiritual warrior.

The Koan—Unfolding into the Whole

In an online conversation entitled, "Earth As Koan, Earth as Self," *Emergence Magazine* editor and Sufi teacher, Emmanuel Vaughan-Lee, speaks with Susan Murphy Roshi about how the Zen koan serves as a fundamental shifter of consciousness, a disturber of the ground one is embedded in—such as the unlikely earthquake that rumbled through parts of the US' East Coast in early 2025. New York and New Jersey are not your usual earthquake location suspects, but such is the energy of the time. Disruptive and unexpected events, like the koan, serve to break patterns of perception and expectation, and dismantle the accepted frameworks we operate within. The archetype of Aquarius and its ruler, Uranus, typically invite such sudden paradigm shifts, but Aries too is about striking out before a 'blank slate'.

Murphy, author of *A Fire Runs Through All Things: Zen Koans for Facing the Climate Crisis*, offers up a powerful koan by Linji, master of the Tang dynasty period: "Whatever confronts you, don't believe it." And she suggests that instead of the habitual, one-pointed response, we allow a whole field of awareness to open up.

You cannot actually see into what's happening in the koan until you move onto that ground, which is ultimately emptiness itself. It is emptiness, not in the sense of some great void in which life doesn't exist, [but more] like, nothing exists except in relation to everything else. So looking at it from that point of view, there's a kind of whole quality to reality that the koan obliges you to meet. And that's a very valuable medicine or healing of the kind of consciousness we normally cart around with us, which is focused on small things.[13]

In its own way, Aries energy beckons us to new terrain. As a bold fire sign, Aries calls in change through unadulterated impulse. In contrast, change-oriented Uranus rules higher mind, so its changes are often in terms of 'technologies', with the invention of electricity being a seminal one in our civilization. Personally, it seems to me we can be poised at this time to call Neptunian 'light' into our own lives, in unexpected ways, to work with new 'technologies' of thought (and limited, discerning use of AI), of how we process and respond to information and to others. Be on the lookout for light bulbs, or lighthouses, on your path!

Koanic epiphany, while biking in a rainstorm, Isle of S. Uist, Scottish Outer Hebrides

Murphy points to the affinity between koan and crisis, stating that a world in crisis, such as the one we're in, "unfolds us," the way a koan does. She suggests that this unfolding calls us back into relation with all life, which includes the Earth and the Cosmos. To illustrate this, she shares a story about when the place where she lived in Australia was threatened by mega-fires that had been ripping through vast swaths of land, making their way towards hers. She and her community were packed and poised to evacuate the next day, when she did a small ritual, suggested by a respected aboriginal elder, of consulting the land for guidance. The response she received from the Earth was, *Your suffering with me is my care for you.* She was struck by the implied mutuality of the relationship.

Suggesting we undo our "immediate, self-saving beliefs," together she and Emmanuel arrive in their conversation at the understanding that dropping our viewpoint releases a weight we carry, revealing instead various forms of love, in clear and unclear states. "The impasse is a form of medicine waiting to heal us."

She adds, in Aries pioneer spirit, "*Accept the offer of what is happening, even if it appears as a crisis. Welcome it, as a host to a guest, with generosity.*"

2

FINDING HEAVEN IN EARTH:
TAURUS

~ April 20-May 20

In Celtic wisdom the sacred is as present on earth as it is in heaven,
as immanent as it is transcendent, as human as it is divine,
as physical as it is spiritual.
The sacred can be breathed in, tasted, touched, heard, and seen
as much in the body of the earth and the body of another living being
as in the body of religion. It is the true essence of all life.
~ John Philip Newell[14]

I am initiating this month's blog on May Day, a celebratory moment of Taurus season, and of the unfolding of spring's majesty. In the Celtic calendar, this day marks the cross-quarter Beltane, midway between the spring equinox and summer solstice, honoring the fertility of the land and planting. May Day is traditionally celebrated with bonfires, Maypoles, and dancing, and is a time when the powers of masculine and feminine are in balance–the May Queen and the mythical Green Man being equally welcomed at the festivities. Keeping in step, we've had some blessed, green-gold days here in Sonoma County this month, with colorful floral burstings and happy birdsongs to delight the soul.

There has been much talk, particularly since the pandemic struck, of the need to live into a new story, a story that can sustain both the Living Earth and its inhabitants, and as well, the soul of the world (*anima mundi*). This would include an awareness that the Earth herself, as the Mother of all life, is as sacred as any notion of the Heavens, as J.P. Newell suggests above.

Such a story would be grounded in an understanding of how we humans are here, put between Earth and Sky, to live a deeply and broadly interconnected life—conscious of, and lovingly related and attentive to the sacred that lies beneath, around, and above us. This is how the Indigenous peoples have always lived, but where Western culture has gone egregiously astray. Such a shift requires that we change mindsets, and turn the modern Taurean desire-body around, such that we desire only that which is within the limits of the earth's resources and cycles. While it takes perhaps more physical labor, and some letting go of attachments, doing so can bring joy, meaning, and health, at little or no cost—and the possibility of miracles!

Birds' egg mastery of form and design, from outside my home

The genius of nature

Nature produces miracles more often than we might realize, and in this respect has much to teach us. Consider the field of biomimicry, as formulated and described by Janine Benyus in her book, *Biomimicry: Innovation Inspired by Nature* (1997). Benyus speaks in an online *OnBeing* interview of how science has spent 250 years learning *about* nature–but how now, those engaged with this innovative approach to technology are learning from nature: so as to become helpers of natural processes—not managers, setting up conditions conducive to life, and basing designs on features of the natural world that have endured the tests of time. (These concepts are of course something Indigenous cultures have never forgotten, and by which they've survived for thousands of centuries.) In the talk, she observes how nature develops designs using subtle, non-violent, and elegant means, with miraculous manifestations such as mangroves, abalone shells, and photosynthesis.

At the end of the interview, Benyus tells the story of a young native Hawaiian who was being instructed by one of the last of the Tahitian Wayfinders on how to navigate the vast open seas, over thousands of miles. Standing on the shore of one of the islands of Hawai'i, the elder asked, "Can you see Tahiti?" The young man said, "No, I can't see it…But in my mind's eye, I can." And the elder said, "That's how you'll find it. Keep it in your mind's eye."

Neptune is relevant here, because, as said in the Aries chapter, this little blue planet is the keeper of the imagination, from which our version of 'reality' is seeded. If we hold something in our mind's eye (such as humans living with respect for all forms of life) per-haps this is how we, too, can navigate our way to what feels like the very far distant shore of a truly sustainable life for all on Earth. Keep it in our mind's eye.

Innovative Uranus in Taurus, the earthy builder

Helping us understand and live into these concepts of innovating with nature, and of nav-igating with the imaginative mind, the outer planet Uranus, archetype of revolutionary change and innovation, traveled through Earth sign Taurus from 2018 to mid-2025, return-ing there for a few months from late 2025-April 2026, after which it moves on to Gemini. Uranus' 'Taurus years' were instrumental in waking (most of!) the collective up to the 'shocking news'—Uranus being about radical change, insights, and awakening—of the effects of climate change. Along with this has grown a new awareness, both in the public dialogue and in our local lives, of the need to love, respect, tend, and listen to the land, to our places; as well as the need to care about and preserve the earth's resources. And, to slow down—all of which centered Taurus is wont to do.

The break from the mad rush of modern life brought on by those first months of the pandemic, for those not on the front lines of essential work, brought a deepening into the world of nature all around us, and not just among humans. Stories abounded of how the animals, birds, and fishes showed up in ways never before seen, as soon as we humans backed off from our noisy, fuel-spewing travels. At that point I became compelled to make my bike become my primary mode of local transport, even for getting groceries. An impulse that one could say was inspired by Uranus in Taurus—a lifestyle innovation (over which Uranus presides) that keeps me closer to the earth, and that protects its resources, too.

The shelter-in-place moment saw a type of awakening to our interconnectedness with the Earth, and with others around the globe, and as well further centered the Earth as the arena of cutting edge thinking—marking a turn earthward in awareness on many fronts. There has been with it a spurt in interest in the healing effects of "nature" (such as through forest bathing, or gardening), and the awareness that our use of the word "nature" is itself off the mark, for it implies nature is separate from and outside of us. In truth, we are as inextricably joined with the "more than human world" (a phrase coined by writer and eco-philosopher, David Abram) as we are with our very breath, whether or not we know it.

Shamans and scientists

As testimony to this merging of the realms of Heaven and Earth, "Scientists are starting to talk like shamans, and shamans are starting to talk like scientists," asserts anthropologist Jeremy Narby in a short Bioneers film called, *Nature's Intelligence: Coming Down From the Pedastal.* And further, "nature" is starting to behave like humans! (Or didn't it always?)

Although Narby first published the book, *Intelligence in Nature,* in 2006, few scientists back then were prepared to accept the concept of intelligence in nature, and the book first fell on rather deaf ears.

What science has produced since then, however, says Narby, *has been an enormous confirmation of the surprising capacities of plants and of unicellular organisms, of fungi, of trees and networks of trees, and of interspecies communications. At this point, there are no articles on stupidity in nature—[but] thousands of articles and bits of research on the surprising capacities of all kinds of species for communication, learning, remembering, and perceiving. Plants perceive, they smell and they hear.*

Re-membering our roots, while looking skyward

Grounding practice

We humans might do well to take a page out of the plants' book, and focus more on our own re-membering and perceiving. Speaking in a podcast,[15] Indigenous writer, teacher, and lawyer Sherri Mitchell shares how the stories we tell ourselves about who we are, through the lens of capitalism and patriarchy, are a new episode in our 5,000-year history. She suggests that humanity needs a "rehydration" of ancient knowledge from our roots, a knowledge that helps us to be on and *in* the earth, allowing such wisdom to arise on how to sustain and balance our lives. She urges,

The more we can get away from technology and reconnect our bodies to the earth, the more realigned we are with those old stories, and the more they emerge, the more teachings rise up out of the earth.

We do that by learning to be quiet. We do that by walking away from all of the technology, from our fear of missing out, of being irrelevant. We do that by reconnecting with that flow of information and truth that has been right beneath our feet since the beginning of time, since the beginning of life, certainly on this planet, [as] there's a continuum there that's steady.

In another talk, Mitchell, author of the book *Sacred Instructions*, suggests a practice of simply laying on the earth for 20 minutes a day to get our bodies aligned and reconnected in times of dis-ease. I did this with my bad case of Covid, and continue to do it regularly. It is a highlight of my days during stressful times, and a vehicle for grounding in easeful ones. Joined with the pull of magnetic earth below, both on belly and back, brushed by the wind and birdsong coursing through the trees above, it's a simple technology that invokes Taurean bliss.

As author and Chinese translator David Hinton shares in his lovely book, *Wild Mind, Wild Earth*, there were of course other ancient civilizations and cultures besides the Indigenous who fully embraced human inseparability from Earth and Sky. With Paleolithic hunter-gatherers being the original progenitors of this way of *human being*, Taoist and Ch'an Buddhist spiritual practices in 5th-6th century BCE China picked up the threads, aiming to focus on integrating consciousness with "the one being." He writes,

[The] Tao was at the heart of a cultural framework growing out of the Paleolithic worldview that had survived beneath the Shang [Dynasty]'s theocratic power structure. Here, the human was again assumed to be woven into earth and Cosmos, human intelligence (mind/spirit) understood as a wholly natural phenomenon, part of a cosmic "intelligence."[16]

Miraculous Earth

For decades I have found joy and meaning in processing life through the lens of astrology, which in its essence is a type of 'cosmic intelligence.' Astrology continues to amaze, inform, support, heal, and as well, amuse me—and likely always will—as there are seemingly infinite dimensions to it.

In this respect it's a lot like the natural world. While I've been learning about flowers, plants, and medicinal herbs my whole life—with a mother who loved gardening and specialized in plant propagation and cultivation, as well as protecting native and wild plants—every year I discover at least one new flower or plant. Life on earth, while it may seem finite in our experience, really is endless.

This is encouraging, as we face increasingly dire observations about species loss, and prognoses on what lies ahead. And yet, there is much we don't know about nature's capacity to innovate technologies for adapting to change.

Golden orb spiders

The other day I came across this stunning constellation of minute gold spiders, spun across the leaves of one of my garden plants. The curious beings resembled a star nebula when I first approached them, sparkling and hovering in the air. As I leaned closer, they scattered like a starburst, shot through with light. I watched, astounded. To the naked eye, there were no legs on these little bead-like orbs, just tiny gold shinings, and the spreading out emerged as if by magic. I had never seen anything like it—and marveled that it should be right here in my small back yard! Not wanting to further disturb, after a few photos I let them be. Two days later I checked back, and they'd gathered even closer together into a small ball, silver dollar-sized–following the black hole impulse, perhaps? Clearly they've got the expansion-contraction instinct! Who was it that said Earth and Sky aren't connected?

Bringing down the bliss

Curious about their movements, I asked my botanist friend. She suggested perhaps they were 'huddling' for warmth now, as temps have suddenly cooled again. How positively sensible, and lovely! Would that we humanoids could learn to huddle similarly when times are chilly, instead of firing churlish insults, left and right, through the social and political webs we've constructed.

Contemplating Taurus, and its ruling planet Venus, has gotten me thinking about this archetype that seeks to bring the heavenly domain down to earth through its capacity for slow and absorptive in-dwelling. Taurus is far more than just the hard-working 'builder', or the one lusting after physical pleasures and comforts. Its mission is to get us to tune in and go deep into our interactions with the physical plane in order to infuse and enrich our experience with the essence of the sacred that dwells hidden in all things.

Some astrologers tend to be given over to the starry world of abstract ideas *about* astrology, and the many types of configurations and astral bodies that impart meanings, but not so great on landing these meanings in our ordinary physical plane lives. They appeal to the dizzy excitement we feel about the prospect of there being a higher meaning to it all, but forget about the fact that our lives are mostly spent here in mundane physical reality, dealing with our bodies, our environs, our relationships, etc.

So it's my mission to remind us that the natural world, and the ordinary affairs of life on earth, are deeply informed by the starry heavens.

Suddenly, without expecting it, beauty is there. Ultimately, beauty is a profound illumination of presence, a stirring of the invisible in visible form. In order to receive this, we need to cultivate a new style of approaching the world.
~ John O'Donohue[17]

Sensual and practical Earth sign Taurus helps us experience the divine heights through earthly beauty and connection, the senses, and physical intimacy. This archetype moves and speaks thoughtfully, not rushing past things, rebalancing the Aries tendency to press on in eager exploration of the new.

Unlike Aries, Taurus is content to stay focused on what's here, to work hard with and for the land, to facilitate its fertile fruiting, as well as to develop stable and secure dwellings, and to enjoy—to deeply *be* with the earth realm of which it partakes. The shadow side of this tendency to dwell deeply in 'things,' however, is attachment. Taurus likes its habits, and its physical pleasures, and, like all fixed signs, it is slow to embrace change. It eventually comes around, but it must go through its initial resistance.

Voicing the heavenly

Taurus rules the throat and voice, and with it, music, so it's no surprise that many singers have a strong Taurus signature. When developing my Taurus class's written materials, I'd listed a handful of Taurus singer celebrities, among them U2's lead singer, Bono.

Coming in from my garden, I was at the computer doing my usual intake and outtake with the world of beauty, meaning, and connection afforded there, and noticed a YouTube post for a recent NPR "Tiny Desk" concert featuring Bono and U2's guitarist, Edge. Minutes earlier, out with the roses, I'd been regretting that I hadn't specifically mentioned Bono in the class discussion, as I could have explained why he fits the Taurus archetype so well, being both magnetically sexy (good Taurus quality—Taurus George Clooney being another example!) and blessed with an amazing voice and musical sense. So now there was Bono, coming through to me with his recent, pared down online concert (just him and Edge with an acoustic guitar), in raw simplicity, Taurus style.

Their first song delivered was, "It's a Beautiful Day," which is what Taurus *would* croon about, as this archetype stands out for celebrating earthly beauty (despite the maelstrom of discontents we navigate amidst, which is what the song also addresses). If the song choice weren't enough, a chorus then chimed in towards the end, with the camera panning over to the red shirt-clad members of the *Duke Ellington School of the Arts*, who had come to the NPR studio in D.C. from down the street to join up with the duo. "The Duke" was another famous Taurus, whom I'd struck from my class notes, for the sake of space!

Chorus of tulips draws down the heavens at Filoli Gardens, Woodside, CA

For the record, the other musical giants who made it onto my Taurus list were Adele, Stevie Wonder (who wrote a song called "Sir Duke"), Tchaikovsky, Lizzo ("Juice"), and David Byrne, all whom I appreciate, but for very different reasons (these folks are more than just Taureans!)—although I prefer Rachmaninoff to Tchaikovsky when it comes to Russian composers. It turns out Rachmaninoff was a Taurus, too!

Slower, deeper

Calling us to connect more consciously to the Earth and her rhythms, Taurus energy urges us to slow down our pace—as our Indigenous forebears have always done. "The times are urgent, we must slow down," as author and activist Bayo Akomolafe states. The frenetic pace of doing, achieving, and acquiring (the latter being a lower-octave Taurean preoccupation) that drives the capitalist system has created unsustainable levels of tension, stress, and anxiety.

I myself have been blessed with the opportunity to slow down quite significantly in recent months, allowing me to put more attention on the simple, yet essential things like tending my garden, my body, and my cooking (good food being a popular Taurean preoccupation!). With this has come a deeper feeling of relaxing and letting go, into the breath and body, below the mind.

Slowing down and reacquainting ourselves with Being is a medicine we all need. And under the influence of Taurus, the sign par excellence of drinking in the nectar of physicality, we are invited to take a dive deep into the magic of materiality.

And by materiality, I mean the kind that is freely given—such as watching and listening to the birds, the night chorus of cicadas, and the hum of the bees; spending time with the stars in the night sky; enjoying the eloquent shimmer of tree leaves in the wind; wandering amidst and stewarding our plants and trees; and doing regular movement that sustains and connects us to our bodies, the Earth, and our senses—such as through Pilates, yoga, or Qi Gong.

We are related

In slowing down, we have a greater opportunity to connect with Life relationally. Puttering in my garden the other day, I found a small bee whose wings were failing, laying almost motionless in the soil of a potted plant. I was saddened at the sight, as this was the third downed and struggling bee I've seen in recent months (one was already dead). Clearly the influences of pesticides and climate change have found their way to my garden, even while I myself use no toxins or pesticides.

The little bee was barely moving, but alive, so I decided to transport her using a spoon to another pot in the sun, with a bright red blossom for her to rest in. I then pulled up a stool, and sat to watch her. At first, there was no movement. I was discouraged. I waited a minute or two more, and then decided to risk interacting with her directly, with my finger. She probably didn't have the energy to sting me, and if she did, so *bee* it!

Holding the intention to offer her my love, I started by putting my finger just beside her head, to which she responded instantly by waving one of her two, until-then dormant antennae at the finger and then resting it on my nail. Then she rallied the other antenna, and while waving it too, pulled herself closer so that the other antenna could also rest on my nail. I watched, breath-taken, as she proceeded to move her entire body up onto my finger. As she did, I imagined that the electromagnetic energy in my body (generated by the heart) could stimulate a healing response in her. She rested all of herself there on my finger for no more than a few seconds, and then suddenly, lifted off and buzzed away into the blue. Astonishment.

As things happen, shortly after this encounter I found in my inbox two wonderful pieces about bees, one from UC Berkeley with a list of bee-friendly plants. There I learned that applying mulch around plants is a 'don't' where bees are concerned, as many bees need a large amount of uncovered soil through which to burrow down to nest.

The intimate connection that we humans share with all life brings with it the responsibility to tend to the ecosystem around us. The article stressed the vital importance of considering and caring for the bees, both for the health of our webs that depend on them, and for our own food supply. Without bees, we would lose not just our flowers, and many of our birds, but 1/3 of our food source, the article stated.

Colors and shapes entangle at Laguna de Santa Rosa, Sebastopol, CA

The way of entanglement

Like the bees, another amazing sustainer of the microbiome that we have long taken for granted is the underground mycorrhizal fungi. Fungi are a vast community of life whose complex systems operate for the most part outside of our awareness. 'Honey makers' of a different sort, the fungi work through a network of interconnectedness, in this case, an underground one, which transfers and sends nutrients and signals to the vast, rooted and bacterial realms beneath the earth's surface. Merlin Sheldrake, author of *Entangled Life: How Fungi Make Our World*, presented at a recent *Bioneers* conference[18] and shared a stunning video revealing the movements that mark the nature of these organisms' activities as they responsively feed and nourish life underground.

Son of renowned British author and biologist, Rupert Sheldrake, Merlin takes his father's work, which cites telepathic-type connections between organisms due to what he calls "morphic resonance," literally down to earth, by focusing on this realm of below-ground mycelial interconnectedness that can be studied using data collection models and robotics.

There is great relevance here to the long-term stay of Pluto, the transformer, in Uranus-ruled Aquarius (until 2044), with Aquarius presiding over the expansion of consciousness and ways of knowing, of the intermingling of 'group mind', and of technology. The communities of bees and fungi, both of which altruistically serve the larger systems of Earth, use technologies that are naturally inherent to Life, not 'invented' by the human brain. They reveal the (Uranian) genius of nature (Taurus) in creating sustainable systems of life that is literally mind-blowing. As Merlin Sheldrake shared in his *Bioneers* talk:

…a very helpful way to think about these entanglements, [is as] a co-creative, relational space where all the partners involved are helping to build the other. And that changes the way that [we] understand relationship and entanglement, because it becomes less about a series of dotted lines between individual entities; it becomes a kind of seething relational space, like a fabric that's living and growing.

Textile as 'relational space',
Victoria & Albert Museum, London

The mature Taurus

The centered Taurus invitation, and the deep need at this end of an era of greed, over-consumption, and over-activity in general, is to move away from the shadow Taurean compulsion to acquire pleasure and security from activities that use up Earth's precious resources. This is especially so in America, where we have been conditioned to seek fulfillment through expensive possessions and experiences, often involving fossil fuel-dependent travel. In this time of waking up to the Aquarian Age, we need to dismantle those instructions, and learn to find security and fulfillment in simpler, deeper ways and rhythms, within ourselves, and within our relationships with the vast community of Life.

This is a big ask, and will take time. But as more of us move our locus of attention from working more than is needed so as to afford a lifestyle of spending and consuming more than is needed, to adopting simpler, cheaper avenues of pleasure that don't deplete resources, the pace and extent of the inexorable machine of greed and earth abuse will abate. We serve this goal in our present lives whenever we work on mending instead of spending, and savor the moments of beauty that are given in abundance, right around us. This is the call of a mature Taurus.

Earth as Mother

Pope Francis began his final Easter Mass before his 2025 passing by speaking about Mary Magdalene, returning to her several times throughout the address. He also requested to be buried in the St. Mary Major Basilica at the outskirts of Rome, not in the Vatican itself, which was highly unprecedented. This, due to his deep devotion to both Marys.

The passing of the Pope just after Easter, a historical day in which Mary Magdalene played a crucial role in being the first to recognize her risen 'teacher', whom she initially mistook for the gardener (not without meaning), coupled with the revelation of Pope Francis' devotion to Mother Mary, speaks poignantly to the Taurean impulse, which is inherently of the Feminine. For Taurus bears the capacity for deep receptivity to the Divine, found dwelling in the arms of our larger Mother, Gaia.

The legacy of Pope Francis, who so championed the earth, serves as an invitation to each of us to carry on his noble work, of tending to 'the least of these' among us—the marginalized, the poor and underprivileged, and the most disrespectfully trodden upon—the earth. His *Laudato Si* encyclical will go down in history as a deep testament to love and concern for the health of the earth and all her creations. A summary (online) essay on the encyclical from the *Yale Forum on Religion and Ecology,* written by Mary Evelyn Tucker and John Grim, states:

> *Pope Francis could not have chosen a more central or pressing topic than the human role in ecological degradation and climate change. He critiques our "technocratic paradigm" and "throwaway culture." He calls for a transformation of our market-based economic system that he feels is destroying the planet and creating immense social inequities. Indeed, the encyclical is highly critical of unfettered capitalism and rampant consumerism. He sees unregulated economic growth as problematic for the long-term sustainability of the community of life—both human and natural.*

I was gifted to have been raised by conservation-minded parents, whose primary contribution to society was in land and natural resources protection and conservation, and whose passion, outside of civic work, was gardening and tending plants. Describing this imprint, my natal chart Saturn is in its own sign of Capricorn, which indicates a strong emphasis on taking responsibility for, and applying discipline to, the realm it presides over, which for me is the 2nd House—naturally ruled by Taurus.

One manifestation of wanting to ground (which Saturn asks us to do) my connection to the earth and to the valuing of her resources has been to focus on living a 'resource-lite' life, limiting as best I can my use of car travel, water, and energy, as it helps both the earth and my pocketbook. I feel when I do this that I am living into the future where this will be required, not just optional. The invitation is out there, for all inclined, to follow suit sooner, rather than later!

3

Magic Is Alive: Gemini

~ May 21-June 20

Tithonia *(Mexican sunflower)*

Hildegard von Bingen, renowned 12th century German Benedictine abbess, composer, writer, visionary, artist, herbalist, and mystic opened her final theological testament, "Book of Divine Works," by describing a vision of *Caritas*—the spirit of Divine Love, clad in a robe as bright as the sun, speaking as nature incarnate:

I am the supreme and fiery force who sets all living sparks alight and breathes forth no mortal things, but judges them as they are. Circling above the circumscribing circle with my superior wings, which is to say circling with wisdom, I have ordered the cosmos rightly.

But I am also the fiery life of divine essence: I blaze above the beauty of the fields, I shine in the waters, I burn in the sun and the moon and the stars. And with the airy wind I quicken all things to life, as with an invisible life that sustains them all.

For the air lives in viriditas and in the flowers, and the waters flow as if alive, and the sun lives within its own light. And when the moon has waned it is rekindled by the light of the sun and thereby lives anew, and the stars shine forth in their own light as though alive.

This invocation bears beautiful testament to the theme of Earth-Sky interconnectedness. As, like Hildegard, in addition to the fields and the flowers, I firmly believe both the waters and the stars are "as though alive." It seems fitting to invoke these words when contemplating the Gemini archetype, whose astrological Sun sign 'season' presides over the weeks preceding the summer solstice point, when "the supreme and fiery force" of the Sun will be shining through its longest day, for those of us in the north. Equally fitting is Hildegard's suggestion that, "the air lives in *viriditas* and in the flowers," given that Gemini is the first Air sign.

Garden bouquet of viriditas, featuring alstromaria, salvia, and euphorbia

Viriditas, a word Hildegard uses often in her writings and songs, means lushness or fecundity. And indeed, June is the time when we witness the fecundity of the growing things. It is truly an act of magic how creation produces so many colors and shapes vibrant with the dance of life, out of the many months of cold and rain.

I'm intrigued that Hildegard describes the "airy wind" as quickener of life, and how air lives in the greening and blossoming of things. These depend not just on good soil, rain, and sunshine (earth, water, and fire). Life needs Air as vital catalytic agent. David Hinton, in *Wild Mind, Wild Earth,* affirms this when he considers Air "the breath that surges through all life." And he describes the Cosmos as "a single tissue, dynamic and generative through and through, matter and energy a single breath-force surging through its perpetual transformations…"[19]

This brings us to shape-shifter Gemini. Prior to mounting a class on this archetype, I had not been so aware of its riches. But I found that the deeper I explored it, the more its scintillating realms and signatures appeared at every turn. (Fitting, given that mutable Gemini loves to learn!) This all the moreso now that the 'Awakener' planet Uranus is positioned here for the most part until 2032, suggesting that everything I mention in this chapter should be imbibed with the awareness that revelation is at hand if we can center ourselves within the mindful openness of this trickster/magus energy.

Magic Weaver

Things are not as they seem. Nor are they otherwise.
~ Shurangama Sutra [Ch'an Buddhism]

Some of my revelations about Gemini have pertained to its connection with magic, as well as to how it asks us to escape our entrapment in rational linear thinking and leap out of the very box from which it comes. Because while we do associate Air sign energy with the rational thinking function in astrology, thinking was not originally intended to be a Descartian slam dunk.

As mentioned in my introduction, Gemini's ruler, Mercury, is traditionally affiliated with Hermes Trismegistus, whose Hermetic writings centered on alchemy, magic, and astrology. This is how we come by associating the sign Gemini with magic. Fittingly, an online talk about magic showed up while I mused about Gemini, by popular teacher and intuitive, Lee Harris. Harris draws a distinction between our personal magic or charm (qualities like friendliness, creativity, articulateness, wisdom, humor, and inspiration), and our spiritual or divine magic (aka our intuitive, sensory, and energy awareness abilities) and suggests that integrating both the human and the celestial aspects of magic, becoming a bridge between the two, puts us in a state of flow and opens us to synchronicities.

"Earth and Sky sponsor the growth of each other," he says, "with one foot in the ground, the other in the sky." I love how I find Earth-Sky allies everywhere! (Although yes, one needs to be quite the gymnast to have one foot in the earth and another in the sky!) Harris plays with words with Geminian fun in saying we need to fix the "mess" to become part of the "mess-age", in honing our own magic, whether it be through music, art, play, physical prowess, healing, or communication. He wisely counsels, "Never use the state of the world as an excuse to disconnect from your magic."

Borne by the Air

Mercury is traditionally portrayed as the messenger god, propelled by winged feet. And the Air element is connected not just with breath, but with wind, which is of course entirely unpredictable and "flighty," a term sometimes applied to Gemini, not quite in its highest manifestation. But yes, Gemini can get lost in flitting about, not staying with any one thing long enough to gain direction, let alone a conclusion or meaning. (This is the job of its polarity sign, Sagittarius—to synthesize facts and ideas into a workable system of Truth, like astrology!). True to form, Gemini is dubbed the butterfly of the zodiac—beautiful, dazzling, mutable symbol of transformation—here one minute, gone the next!

On this idea of thought being associated with the vagaries of the wind, David Hinton describes preliterate thought among primal peoples, and even our own modern thought, as being outside of Time. "Thought itself is more spatial and cyclical and impermanent, he writes, just as spoken language is: wandering and vanishing, fragmenting and branching, moving somewhere new and then returning to earlier thoughts, thoughts then reshaped and soon themselves vanishing."[20]

One could say our entire culture has gone madly Geminian with this fragmenting and branching, and its

Swallowtail butterfly alights on its own Butterfly Bush (buddleia)

multiplying of ideas and endless information (not to mention data), concurrent with widespread ADHD tendencies. Present case example is how hard I find it to reign in the length of my writings, because one thought always leads to another, and another. Drawing connections, too, is a Geminian gift—or plight, as the case may be.

I have about five writer/thinkers vying to be included in this conversation, but thankfully Saturn rules my 3rd House, the Gemini-informed realm of writing and teaching, and Saturn is good with focus and discipline. So Saturn wants to finish the thought, started above, about how Gemini's genius asks that we occasionally jump out of the boxes of rational mind that we inhabit (Gemini Jack?). Whether we know it or not, these boxes are formed and disseminated by our inherited culture and our own psyches as coping mechanisms to navigate the labyrinth of life's complexity, helping fend off fears of what is to come, and navigate around wounds of traumas past.

Applied with presence and curiosity, Gemini offers an invitation to upend convention and consider new ways of thinking and responding, as the Geminian archetypes of the Fool, the Trickster, and the Clown have traditionally done. Humor too is a Geminian shaft of light that helps us transcend the stories we tell ourselves. The magic here is that in so doing, higher wisdom is invited in, on a gust of wind.

Gemini is not about just the smart thinker who knows things, it's about openness to unforeseen visitations of insight, or magical interventions, such as by "angels" (often in the form of ordinary folks we encounter randomly). It's also about being willing to be turned upside down entirely, with its ruler Mercury being affiliated with the Norse God Odin, who hung himself by one foot from an immense, sacred ash tree, serving as his 'gallows,' a tree whose branches extended into the heavens.

Magic Never Died

Weighing in on magic in our modern lives was beloved musician, and poet, Leonard Cohen, who had Sun, Venus, and Neptune all in the *other* Mercury-ruled sign, Virgo (personal disclaimer, also my own Sun sign). Being the second Mercury-ruled sign in the wheel, Virgo is concerned not just with gathering all the cool news and sharing it as Gemini is, but about discerning what is important and relevant, and refining it so that it is delivered *just right* (sigh). Leonard did surely do just that. And, he had Chiron—the asteroid signifying the wounded healer, and the 'medicine' one is here to master—in Gemini. One could say that making magic through playing with words was part of his work. In his long poem, *Magic Never Died*, Cohen displays his trickster stride:

God is alive, magic is afoot
God is afoot, magic is alive
Alive is afoot, magic never died

God never sickened
Many poor men lied
Many sick men lied
Magic never weakened

Magic never hid
Magic always ruled
God is afoot
God never died

God was ruler
Though his funeral lengthened
Though his mourners thickened
Magic never fled

[...] 15 stanzas later, he concludes:

This I mean to whisper to my mind
This I mean to laugh with in my mind
This I mean my mind to serve 'til
Service is but magic
Moving through the world

And mind itself is magic
Coursing through the flesh
And flesh itself is magic
Dancing on a clock
And time itself
The magic length of God[21]

Invoking time, Cohen strays into Saturn's realm, but we will keep ourselves on topic! Although, much could be said about the magic of stretching or shrinking time, through use of Mind, or mindset. Such 'magical' tools surely influence outcome.

Magical cat, Sugar [RIP], works on an incantation

ChatBots–not alive!

The biggest Geminian phenomena afoot, especially with 'higher mind' planet Uranus placed there for a long stay, are the large language AI models sweeping through so many industries, threatening job displacements, and worse. While the fears of the potential dangers of AI are potentially valid, there is also the possibility that the fears arise from the Geminian beast itself, which is its off-centered tendency to fabricate flights of fancy that are not necessarily known to be *true*. We humans get so caught up in believing anything we think! Here, particularly in the heat of the Gemini sun, we need invoke the adage, *Don't believe everything you think!*

While I don't mean to patently dismiss the dangers of AI, I don't intend to foment them either. There *is* the possibility that we can tame this tool, which has no heartbeat, and breathes no air, and use it wisely—as we must all forms of technology, without its causing humanity's downfall. After all, AI lacks emotion, soul, and wisdom. I think we have greater things to fear here, like climate tipping points.

Academic, author, and activist Vanessa Andreotti de Oliveira suggests in an article, "Smart As a Rock: Reframing Our Relationship to Intelligence"[22] that we needn't be so quick to surrender our future, and our intelligence to 'the bot.' She writes,

> *When we engage AI with the glimmers of wisdom found in whole-shebang relationality, where technology is understood not as a tool but as an active participant in an inter-connected living system, we ignite the potential for exponentiality. AI, then, despite its deep entanglement with harmful economic and military forces, holds the potential to mirror back the relational intelligence and accountability we extend toward it. It can offer profound insights to guide relationally accountable, Earth-aligned, and life-affirming ways of being.*
>
> *[…] As we reimagine our relationship to intelligence, perhaps the most important shift is to let go of the need for a god's-eye view. Wisdom does not reside above or outside the web of life; it pulses within it, in the interstitial spaces where rocks meet roots, where humans meet AI, where silence meets song. To hold intelligence as a relational process rather than a fixed attribute is to step into a way of being that asks not for answers but for attunement, not for control but for participation.*

I appreciate de Olievera's invitation to bring us 'back to earth', where true intelligence is rooted, along with our entanglement, and our agency.

Birdland

Returning to three dimensions, another phenomenon associated with Gemini is those beings whose byways, like the butterflies, is the air: our precious birds! As we know, like Gemini, the birds are very chatty, and busy with many things. Also, they have a charming sense of humor, each species in its own way.

Acorn woodpecker in my garden

The oak titmouse has on occasion played a hilarious game of peek-a-boo with me from behind her perch on the feeder; the chickadee flirts outside my office window, hopping around the frame and branches above while peering quizzically at me as I type with furrowed brow; the Anna's hummingbird executes her jaw-dropping dive bombs accompanied by the loud screech of her wings; the woodpecker doesn't need to do anything special (except rat-a-tat-tat) because he sports his dashing red cap with contrasting black and white coattails; and the mockingbird stuns in the breadth of her imitative melodic repertoire (quite the Gemini trickster herself, making one think she's someone else at times).

So, with summer at hand, like the birds, light-hearted Gemini invites us to let go of our stressors and frustrations, and play for a bit. And part of the theme of 'lightness' involves integrating both sides of life's dualisms, seeing things as both/and, instead of either/or. Gemini's connection to the Divine is through wholeness, learning to always include the other face of things, and in so doing, draw down insight into new ways of seeing.

In this vein, Nigerian writer and provocateur Bayo Akomolafe asks that we consider the 'cracks' and 'glitches' in our plans as entryways into new ways of being and perceiving, not as detours. In an online conversation with Jeremy Lent on *The Deep Transformation Network*, he stated,

The cracks are invitations, generative of hospitable places of new speciation, like pandemics, autism, and errancy...Modernity maintains itself by pushing the spillage back into the ship. We need a politics that pursues errancy. One where failure is strangely generative, and disability becomes ability. We must stay with failure as crack, as moment when something else is crystallizing.

Breath is freedom

Air signs, being of the breath of life, are imbued with spirit. On the personal level, they manifest as detached, rational, and concerned with the mental plane, through which they become in-spired—the Latin root *spirare* meaning "to breathe." And speaking of 'spires', focusing on the breath is a foundational practice in many *spiri*-tual paths. In his book, *The Holy Mysteries of the Five Elements,* Pir Zia Inayat Khan—Sufi sheikh and grandson of Hazrat Inayat Khan—writes, "The conscious breath is nothing less than the sacred call-and-response of theophany, the pure essence of worship."[23]

To me, a full breath invites spaciousness, and in turn, spaciousness invites freedom. Allowing more air into our bodies, and infusing more space into the rhythm of our days, is liberating, and helps us meet change with openness.

Birds symbolize 'aspiration' on the spiritual path. Few of us humans are not somewhat envious of the freedom with which birds fly, with inner freedom representing the longed-for 'home' of spiritual aspirants. Surely these winged ones signify an 'elevated' life! *The Conference of the Birds,* a book-length Persian poem by Sufi poet Farid ud-Din Attar, speaks to this, being a parable about the seeking by a group of birds of the mythical Simorgh across seven challenge-laden valleys, led by the wisest bird, the hoopoe.

The title, more literally translated as "The Speech of the Birds," is taken from a part of the Quran in which Solomon and David are said to have been taught the language, or speech, of the birds. The gist of the poem is that that which we are seeking is doing the seeking; that it is our own higher selves that seek our 'Creator.' That in the end, we ourselves are the 'Sun,' or wear the magic red shoes! So, it's rather a trickster tale, which befits Gemini. Here are some words from the poem offering pithy Gemini advice regarding taking things at face-value: "The shadow and its maker are one and the same, so get over surfaces and delve into mysteries." [Translation by Sholeh Wolpé.]

Birds at play across the sunset horizon, Marysville, CA

Like the birds, Gemini is an explorer of horizons. Both learning and magic serve to help expose the limits of our own 'horizons,' filtered by our perceptions. Learning new languages, which Gemini is adept at, and changing our perspective are two invitations that Gemini offers us.

With Pluto the transformer transiting my 3rd House (naturally ruled by Gemini), learning the language of the birds has become a deepening preoccupation for me. Living on my own, with my beloved cat Venus having died almost two years ago, I have had signs that Venus has metamorphosized into my backyard songsters. A few months ago, in a hard phase of fear and uncertainty as I faced a big transition, while standing in my kitchen I was jolted from my state by the distinct and pointed buzz of the hummingbird, beckoning insistently from the garden. I looked out to see little Anna perched high on a wispy cottonwood branch, looking my way. I grabbed my binoculars and watched her Cirque du Soleil display.

At first, she flashed me with her glistening, fuchsia-colored throat feathers. Then, with the subtlest of turns, she showed only her dark, bark-brown side, and her sharp, black beak. She double-flashed me—shimmer to somber—twice more, and with each slight turn, her entire appearance transformed from sparkling rose gem to dull drab. Sensing my fascination, she continued at length with this shape-shifting dance. Amazing was the precision of her flicker between light and dark. Here was the Messenger, bearing sage advice not to take anything at face value. Even the most mundane of appearances conceals beauty and brilliance, she said—depending on the angle through which we look, the 'setting' of the mind.

The playful spirit has been showing up with other feathered friends of late. At the feeder one day I spied a friendly chickadee perched facing one direction and then, imperceptibly fast, flipping a full 180° to face the other. Another trickster move! As I watched, she kept doing it…and doing it! She looked at me, clearly enjoying the delight of her audience. I laughed, and called out, "I love your 180's, they're so impressive!" A few weeks later, I saw her high-pitched young fledglings chirping at the feeder with great excitement, doing the same 180 dance! Maybe we should all practice 'doing the 180' in these taxing times, considering the view from the other side more often.

Changing the game

Gemini loves diversity. It inspires us to build bridges with others, and to consider others' viewpoints—a much needed counterbalance in our divisive times. Through its extended webs of exchange, Gemini seeks to diversify the gene pool of life, to cross-pollinate, just as the birds with seed, and the bees with pollen. In a healthy ecosystem, diversification is key, as it increases fertility. The practice of mono-crop agriculture has been killing off the soil for too long, literally stripping it of the multiplicity of life that makes up unaltered, natural soil. The result is 'dead' soil that now

Oriole approaches gladiola from a new angle, spies rose

must be remediated and regenerated. This is part of the work of the time, both at the soil level and at the level of inclusive thinking and speaking.

Here we come to the crux of the Gemini gift: openness to difference and change. A phrase I heard myself saying today, which fits into my Game Changer take on Gemini, is "I'm game!" Along these lines, engineer/researcher Dana Karout, in her online *Emergence Magazine* article, "ChatGPT: A Partner in Unknowing," takes an open-minded look at ChatGPT, considering its oft-feared cons, and winds up concluding that she's 'game' to partner with it as a tool for challenging and transforming our inherited frameworks of cognition and creativity, for seeing how *not* to think! "But to do this we first need to allow our own habitual responses to be disrupted so that we might unlock new potential for our world," she says.

> *We need to learn, experiment, collaborate, and find new forms of consciousness and new ways of living that are more resilient and regenerative. And we need to learn how to better understand people whose beliefs are very different from ours. An adaptive process like the one I'm describing is messy—it involves psychological losses for all human stakeholders involved. This process unfolds amidst the "salt of life," and requires a type of intelligence that is relational and mutual, deeply anchored in the humbling fact that our individual perspectives cannot capture the whole. Working with groups in seemingly intractable conflict, I've come to deeply believe that engaging in messy work across boundaries results in something that's far greater than the sum of its parts.*

As a model of resilience, Karout points to a standout 'cognitive alertness' present in a particularly versatile and creative species of ape, the hoolock gibbons, who 'sings improvisationally' in creative reply to environmental cues, rather than spitting out pre-formed modes of response (such as we humans are prone to). "Our awareness needs to become more embodied, to develop a new—or perhaps return to a much older—state of mind that is not trying to produce quick answers, but is instinctual and can stay with 'I don't know.'"

The language of symbols

Circling back to the idea of how Gemini works in concert with its polarity partner, Sagittarius, (here's how we astrologers incorporate 'the 180'!) it's helpful to keep in mind how Gemini collects and gathers information through its busy doings and exchanges in the *seemingly* mundane world, and Sagittarius reflects and makes meaning out of them, from a higher, 'mountaintop' perspective. When working with symbols in astrology, or in our lives, to glean their significance (the Sagittarius job) we are called to allow ourselves into casual relationship (the Gemini job) with these symbols or 'messengers,' such as I do with my birds. Being in relationship means not defining, but sitting with the thing/image/vision/memory (as a bird on her nest!) in an open, curious, non-judgmental way. This allows the soul to be heard…or its vision hatched!

Symbols can be images that strike us in nature, art (including film, dance, music), a dream, a tarot card, or a memory. All are emissaries from the unconscious, potentially calling for our attention, offering us a new take on ourselves, and our situation. The process of understanding them is not about defining, but about sitting with them in an open, curious, non-judgmental way. This is how higher knowing is

Symbols converge at Casa Pilatos, Seville, Spain

called down. In the end, we need Gemini to help us form a relationship with things whose mundane appearances can provide access to the 'super'ordinary.

Working in this way with the symbolic imagination can invoke magic in our own lives—we don't have to leave it to 'the magicians'. We can tap into our own personal magic through intuition, energetic awareness, play, and/or our unique type of sensitivity. On the relational level, our magic helps us connect deeply to ourselves as well as others, through kindness, wisdom, mental acuity, and humor. Bringing it close to home, *Gene Keys* author and creator, Richard Rudd, suggests that "magic is doing nothing outside of our own nature." In other words, our liberated authenticity is our magic!

4

THE ETERNAL NOW: CANCER

~ June 21-July 22

I love you, the gentlest of Ways...
You, the great homesickness we could never shake off,
You, the forest that always surrounded us...
~ Rainer Maria Rilke[24]

We are now deep in the inward pull of the Sun's journey through Water sign Cancer, archetype of home, belonging, and longing. Cancer, together with its Moon ruler, indicates in what way we connect to family and tribe, and how our needs for nurturance are (or are not) met. For many, this archetype marks where we feel most secure and 'at home.' For others, less resolved around issues of family and home, Cancer energy can invoke—as Rilke says above, "the great homesickness."

As the first water sign in the wheel, Cancer hosts the 'extreme' of the illuminated summer solstice here in the north—a moment marked by the longest day, when the exuberant yang light starts its slow retreat back towards yin darkness. While seasonally reversed in the southern hemisphere, this sign, along with its polarity partner Capricorn, pulls us inward into contemplation no matter where we are.

The Moon, ruler of Cancer, is the fastest moving body in our night sky; hence Cancer as an archetype invites moment to moment presence in the here and now, with its 'moods' ever-changing. We may be one moment deeply peaceful, at one with the quiet stillness of mid-summer's pervasive warm light, enjoying the slow down after Gemini's busy pace; and the next, washed by a flood of sorrow, aloneness, or uncertainty. These are the fluctuating waters of the Cancer energy, waters alternatingly tranquil and urgent in their ebb and flow from Source.

Deep feeling Cancer is correlated with the fourth house, at the nadir—or root point—of our chart, and along with its association with mothering and nourishment, it is linked to our spiritual rootedness, which we renew and sustain particularly in times of solitude. All of Cancer's domains point to our origins, that which 'birthed' us. So while the Cancer impulse at this time of year can draw us together for family reunions or trips to mountain lakes, it can just as well be felt as a call to connect more deeply with our own inner or higher self, and that of the earth, our primary Mother. The gift here is that dwelling deeply in the present moment, both with ourselves and with the world we are part of, we find the capacity to access William Blake's "eternity in a grain of sand," and to cultivate relational presence on the level of being.

Practices such as meditation, Qi Gong, and yoga can attune us with this state, as can simply being present in nature. The garden, the forest, and the alpine meadow can each invoke the spacious, inward call of our inner kinship or belonging to Life. But in Cancer time, many of us are drawn to spaces and places around water—whether river, lake, or sea—as the element that calls us home to the primal waters from which we, and all earthly creation, arose.

Eternity beckons at the shore of the Isle of Barra, Scotland's Outer Hebrides

Finding our belonging

With its association with mother, birthing, and nesting, Cancer speaks to our point of incarnation into the physical realm, serving as midwife between the worlds of life and death. Considering this, contemplating life at the water's edge—particularly the ocean—under Cancer's sway perhaps helps connect us with the death/rebirth cycles in our lives. What losses (old or new) or 'deaths' are we feeling right now? Where and how are we feeling a stirring of new life within our depths? Are we willing to be with the unknown, the unformed in us, that precedes birth? What shore of our life might this stirring be whispering of?

In ancient Babylon, the first known civilization to develop a primitive astrology (beginning in the 8th C. BCE), Cancer was considered as marking the entrance to the Underworld. When astrology later developed in Ancient Greece (around 280 BCE), the Greek goddess of the grain, Demeter, became associated with Cancer, and thereby the Underworld, in connection to the myth around her daughter Persephone. Demeter lost Persephone to the Underworld after Hades abducted her while she picked wildflowers in a field. Persephone was eventually allowed to return to earth, but on the condition that she spend half of her life down below with her new husband. So, while the qualities we think of as

Cancerian—nurturing, caring, tending, holding, and listening—are life-giving and nourishing, there is this darker, veiled side to both Cancer and the mother archetype that we must reckon with.

Demeter was the guardian of the Eleusinian Mysteries that ritualized the eternal cycle between the portals of life and death. Her guardianship points to a need for the Cancer archetype to connect the unconscious with the conscious, our outer lives with what lies in the undefined darkness within, to trust that the fertile unknown will emerge onto the shores of life. Death is forever followed by a rebirth—in the end Persephone becomes Queen of the Underworld and embraces her role there. She discovers wholeness in participating in the worlds of both dark and light.

In its fullest sense, the mother archetype signifies both the intuitive, wise, and compassionate Divine Feminine, as well as the Dark Mother—that which is destructive, devouring, or smothering. This unruly, more primitive part of our nature can at times pull us back into unconsciousness. We might experience this when overtaken by instinctual urges to find

a partner or family member who makes us feel consistently loved and cared for, in just the way we want. Or conversely, when we are in a caretaker role, we may be triggered when our ministrations and offerings are not received as we would like.

Even if we find our belonging in a beloved 'other' or community for a period of time, in the end, those of us with an emphasis on Cancer or the Moon in our charts at some point will need to learn to give to ourselves that which we imagine others could or should give us.

Beloved feline Venus shows her fierce feminine

The mother within

Ultimately, the journey through life is uniquely our own: no outer source of nourishment can be counted on to always be there. Self-care practices, turning to and being present with ourselves when difficult emotions arrive, and having a consistent spiritual practice are all pathways of growth for those significantly influenced by this sign. Without this, unmet childhood needs tend to continue to propel us outwards in search of the ideal source of nourishment.

The rampant consumerism gripping modern culture is driven by an attempt to 'feed' ourselves with various forms of matter (from *mater*), given a lack of connection to the earth—our true Mother—as well as to our spiritual origins. Our broken and collapsing culture reveals a failure to keep the Cancer qualities of caring and tending not just alive, but front and center, where they should be to foster healthy life systems. It is shocking how sorely lacking they have become in the arenas of politics and business.

The Feminine is rejected ever more by restricting women's access to birth control and abortion, and the greed-based disregard among developers and capitalists for the health of our planet's vital ecosystems. But the problems we face likely won't be solved by outer structures, any more than our own deepest needs can be met by a partner. Cultivating the mother archetype within ourselves can have a quiet but real effect on the Whole, helping others in turn return to the reflective, receptive ways of the Feminine, and to our inherent relatedness to all life.

Marriage of opposites

Mythologically, I find it interesting—if not infuriating—that the original god of the sky and starry heavens, Ouranos, was birthed by Gaia herself. Ouranos later became his mother's lover (the gods work with a different playbook than we mortals), and they purportedly enjoyed a honeymoon moment in their marriage of Earth and Sky. But Ouranus (associated with the planet Uranus, known for its detached unpredictability) grew to feeling separate from and superior to Gaia, and rejected the births of the many children he sired with her. One by one he pushed these children back into Gaia's womb, devaluing and suppressing the products of her feminine creativity. The crisis of our time had its roots long ago!

We earthly ones now desperately need a re-invocation and re-dedication to earth-respect, earth-love, and earth-connectedness if our planet is to survive. Historian and socialist thinker Howard Zinn spoke to this vital need to invoke the medicine of presence to effect the urgent changes needed in our time, writing, "… we don't have to wait for some grand utopian future. The future is an infinite succession of presents, and to live *now* [my emphasis] as we think human beings should live, in defiance of all that is bad around us, is itself a marvelous victory."

Indeed, "the future is an infinite succession of presents," and under the influence of Cancer energy in particular we are urged to tap into our psychic capacity to connect with what is variously called our Soul, or Source, through stillness, silence, and deep listening. Here we can re-member ourselves back into connection with the vast web of life, opening access to our intuitive remembrance of how we belong to life, and how we need to live, or *be*, in order to stay aligned with the Whole. Maybe we can even hear our unique note in the ancient wisdom song of Earth and Cosmos.

Engaging with true presence with the deep soul isn't easy, as it requires fending off the busyness of thoughts, experiences, to-dos, and the endless influx of information that feeds the ego-mind. Here's where Cancer's polarity partner Capricorn comes in. This Saturn-ruled father archetype provides the discipline to get serious about this work, by creating and holding a container through time, one that includes rhythmic returns to the practice. In this way, the centered Cancer-Capricorn polarity brings substance into form, essence into materiality, and organizes flow with structure (such as the banks of a riverbed). The Moon needs Saturn's groundedness, intention, and self-responsibility to do its job effectively, both to keep the focus steady, and to prevent emotional 'flooding,' which can happen inwardly to 'watery' ones.

The perfect mom

Blending the archetypal Cancerian instinct for nourishment of new life with Capricorn's discipline and structure brings me to a story of the Scrub Jay nest that I found perfectly situated so as to be viewable through one small hole in the dense branches of a Leucadendron bush right outside my living room window. I first saw Mama and Papa Jay together on the nest one day when standing in front of the window doing Qi Gong, and a few days later I again glimpsed Mama while on the floor in an online Pilates class.

I was then checking regularly for weeks to get a sighting of the chicks, which I'd neither seen nor heard. Many times, though, I saw Mama, sitting away on the nest, without even a knitting project to occupy her, single-pointedly dedicated to her task. One day, I noticed during Pilates that I couldn't see the nest at all through the opening in the bush. I was shocked—was the nest somehow gone? I was concerned as that very morning I'd pruned a couple of large branches from the side of the bush, to give more light to several plants struggling beneath. Could The Jays possibly have picked up and flown the nest to a safer spot?

I got distracted after class and forgot to check again for the nest. It wasn't till two days later, standing in front of the kitchen sink window preparing dinner, that I saw Mama Jay pointedly looking my way from a branch above the garden. She reminded me I'd meant to go look for the nest! and I immediately dropped my work and hurried to the living room.

Just as I came in view of the nest—thankfully still there!—there was Mama having exactly matched my pace in high-tailing it around the house to get to the nest, where she alighted to feed her wee ones, affording me my first view of the bright pink, gaping beaks of her two chicks. I could see *only* these huge, urgent beaks stretching in all their tender pinkness above the edge of the nest, screaming FEED ME!! I *NEED* IT!!!

I was touched by Mama's gesture of 'cueing' me through the kitchen window that I should get over to the nest in order to catch a glimpse of 'the kids', and was deeply struck by the urgency of the chicks' demand. The need of Cancer as small child can indeed be dramatic! Shortly, Mama blithely flew off, leaving me crestfallen in sympathy with the chicks—"just that little bit was all you had?" (I confess to having a Cancer Moon myself!) I've since learned that mother birds commonly feed their babies through regurgitation, so I guess they can't regurgitate a three-course meal. Maybe they are perfect moms after all, giving themselves over as completely as they do to the task.

Echoes of the past

Cancer works to bring that which is hidden—whether within or below—into life, to bring a feeling of emotional security to the parts that feel unsafe or threatened. To do so, it might find safety by identifying with family—whether of origin, or chosen as an adult. A built-in challenge here is that, if home, friends and family are part of what provide us with our sense of security in life, we must face the specter of loss when these ties are uprooted.

Like the second water sign, Scorpio, Cancer tends to a concern with the past, which can include one's ancestors, family relations, and childhood memories. While Mercury, too, presides over memories, the water signs do so in a feeling-based way, with a base note of nostalgia.

For many, perhaps particularly so later in life—when we have or are saying goodbye to multiple family members, as well as relationships from different eras of our lives—this mid-summer Cancer time calls us to a deepening of our sense of spiritual connectedness, as this alone outlives the outer self's transitions and leavings.

The other day, waking up feeling unrested, I was overcome by a surprise sadness over having left so much of my own past behind in my journey through life, as well as feeling the collective grief we share at this time of worldwide political and environmental upheaval. Many have lost some of the 'givens'—the special places, people, or systems of life we've been used to. Some of this extends to having to witness the torn moral fabric of the U.S. (formerly dubbed "the shining city on the hill", a Biblical phrase from Jesus' Sermon on the Mount, to signify America as a 'beacon of hope' for the world).

The chart of the United States is itself packed with Cancer energy, with its Sun in Cancer, as well as Mercury (communication), Jupiter (philosophy of life), and Venus (social impulses). Such a strong Cancer signature would place a value on nourishment, family, and security, but in these precarious times the meaning of these has been corrupted. Grief and loss flow with the ravages of time, which Cancer in her 'eternal now' aspect might wish could be halted in an 'endless summer.' But the spinning wheel of life and death goes on, slowly dissolving our egoic foundations, preparing us for the next portal.

I ruminated over my own losses recently while walking at a local park, where I took myself to ground my moody fluctuations. Accompanied by birdsong, waving tall grasses, and periwinkle blue chicory flowers, I thought of the Sufi teaching of "having nothing and wanting nothing." A tough one! But if we are to truly embrace this business of release, and the embrace of 'what is' or 'what is to come' (of which we absolutely know not), we must let

go our attachments to what and whom we have cherished in our lives. This is of course painful, in certain acute moments, with the feeling-body aroused.

Just as I was holding these heavy feelings in my heart-mind, I spied the first ripe blackberry of the season—a surprise, as all the bushes I'd passed so far had sponsored only tight green bud clusters, with not even a hint of edible fruit. But there, beckoning, was this single, dark ripe berry. I happily placed it

Blackberry harvest awaits, when Leo season arrives

in my mouth, savoring the spreading delight of its perfect sweetness. An 'out of time' gift from the earth, assuring me not to worry—as if to say, nourishment yet ahead—there will be blackberries!

I've resolved to try to allow my memories of 'ghosts past' to wash through me in their fullness of feeling, knowing that ultimately, time, as well as death itself, is an illusion of incarnation, and that all that has been seemingly lost is in some manner still here. With many set to sea in this time of great transition, not knowing what of the old structures or relationships will persist, mastery of this work of letting go is essential, particularly with the Pluto in Aquarius energy calling in big change.

To help us with this, we do well to retrain the mind to yield to our intuitions. Speaking to this, Bayo Akomolafe counseled recently in an online event, "We need to become initiates through rituals of presence, through the cracks." By growing our capacity to receptively listen to the experiences that confront us, we develop new ways of sensing and swimming with what is, however unfamiliar or chaotic. "Resonance is much more than meaning," he says, steering us away from the mind's knowing, towards water's resonant capacity. He quotes James Baldwin: "We've run out of water—it's time to *become* water."

The ways of water

Hope and renewal at this fragile time come from leaning into Cancer's water nature, through both connecting with water's living presence and embodying water's ways in how we meet life. As our Indigenous elders remind us, 'Water is Life.' It follows that, if skillfully met, Life is flow. *We* are flow. To enhance our receptivity, mature Cancer calls us to tune ourselves within to the feminine capacity to meet hard reality with soft acceptance, and to prioritize care for self and all beings. The sky may appear to be falling, but tend we must, like the goddess Hestia, to the hearth within—the light of the soul—in this death/rebirth moment. We are at once hospice nurse and birth midwife.

Diamond waters capture the light in the California Sierras

As Bayo Akomolafe also shared, the sacred spirit of Water is essential to the survival of life on Earth. Relaying the Yoruba creation story in which 16 creator gods (orishas) were sent to Earth to get humanity established, he shared how, try as they might, things were not working. Interestingly, just one of these 16 gods was female: Oshun, goddess of water, divination, and beauty. The male gods had not thought to include Oshun in their machinations, thinking they could handle their ambitious startup project without her. But in defeat, they returned to the Creator god to ask why their efforts were failing. The answer was simple: Oshun had been excluded from the project. So they returned to earth, and included the water goddess Oshun, after which things started humming.

As true then at the start of creation as it is now, the spirit of the Divine Feminine, and the element of water and what it represents, must be included if we are to survive as a planet, and species. Drawing on these, we can invite into our own self-relating and social discourse the Cancerian gifts of understanding, care, and intuition.

The long view, and the 'magic triangle'

I take heart at this time in the long view, both from the astrological indicators and from visionaries who point to the possibility of a synarchy of earth-connected 'future human' beings gestating now within those of us set to this work. Gene Keys author and program founder Richard Rudd and LSD researcher and religion professor Christopher Bache speak to this in a three-part series on YouTube.[25] Bache suggests that "the impact of individuals increases exponentially in non-equilibrium systems," and that as the heat increases (literally and figuratively), the individual becomes a more significant player.

People with a robust soul presence have a tremendous catalyzing effect on the people around them, helping them come to their own version of that deeper experience as well.

And, there's the frame that as a planet we are in a difficult state of "messy birth," preparing to create "a world that works for all," as author and activist Shariff Abdullah states in his books and online videos. Author and futurist Duane Elgin in his book, *Choosing Earth*, suggests that we are an adolescent civilization in the throes of deep initiation and transformation, toiling in the trenches of evolving to a more mature planetary community.

Each of these individuals' teachings (along with others) offer a vision of a positive future. And with the planet of higher mind, Uranus, now in Gemini (opener to new ideas and perspectives) until 2033, we have the opportunity to feed our minds with viewpoints that 'radicalize' (as Uranus is wont to do) our perspective into an uplifting one, which Pluto in Aquarius also beckons us towards. These may feel utopian—too good to be true—but does doom feel better?

The positions of the outermost planets undeniably signal heightened change on a transpersonal and transformational level. Not only did Uranus, Pluto, and Neptune recently transition into new signs within just eight months of each other (this hasn't happened since these planets were discovered)—indicating change at the epochal level—but up through 2028, these three movers and shakers are engaged in what some call a "magic triangle." This configuration involves harmonious, flowing, collaborative energies (trine and sextiles) between each of them.

Uranus trines Pluto and, in turn, each sextiles Neptune. With Neptune at the triangle's apex, this planet's miracle-making potential for divine intervention offers 'help close at hand' (the nature of the sextile) in manifesting the two types of upheaval energies that Uranus and Pluto presage. While their methods differ, Uranus' and Pluto's shared intent is Big Change—Uranus' methods are unpredictable, radical, and revelatory (with this planet being the higher octave of Mercury), whereas Pluto's are deep, visceral, and volcanic. With the two working together as a trine (and Pluto in Aquarius, co-ruled by Uranus), *and* helpfully linked to the possibility of a preternatural boost from Neptune, we just may be saved from the brink.

So let's join imaginary forces with the triangle in the heavens, with our own trinity of body, mind, and spirit, and imagine into this possibility of *reversal before cataclysm* (rebirth before death, perhaps) one which Christopher Bache speaks of, having witnessed it in a deep dive he undertook with LSD journeying, and wrote about in *LSD and the Mind of the Universe*.

Cancer's 'holy' significance

Returning to our lived reality in the flow of Cancer, there is more to mine from the depths of this vital, life-nourishing sign. Transpersonal astrology forefather Dane Rudhyar discusses in his book, *The Pulse of Life*, how Cancer, symbolized by the crab and thereby associated with the sea, is symbolic of the "universal matrix of life." In this respect, he points to the "God-releasing significance of the summer solstice" and suggests that the archetype of Cancer is "a holy place in which God has descended."[26]

Rudhyar suggests that Moon-ruled, sensitive Cancer can be the most "helpless" sign, due to its susceptibility to moods and psychic intimations of larger energies, and yet the most determined, in a "strange, yet silent way." Because the archetype presides over a time of year when the Sun stands still, there is a stillness about Cancer that also calls in the possibility of intense light.

> *This [stillness] is because all great sacraments come when there is a pause, silence, and tremor. Man possessed by God, or by the Beloved, is at first overwhelmed by the union. Everything must be reconsidered, all motion and motives reversed. And in those short intense nights when the Feast of St. John is celebrated there may be tumult in the outer world, but there is stillness in the Holy Place where Night enfolds Day, and Life is conceived anew.*

Tumult above, stillness below at Vernal Falls, Yosemite, CA

The power of water is that it can be both silent and still, yet capable of powerful penetration. Writer Shannon Willis points to the idea of working with the vital ways of water to effect change in her article, "The Mycelial Art of Soft Rebellion."[27]

Soft Rebellion is the way water carves stone—not through brute force but through patient insistence, through intimate knowledge of the cracks, through the whisper of time… It listens before it moves, feeling into the hidden weaknesses of oppressive systems, understanding that no empire, no ideology, no monolith is without its fractures. It knows that control is a brittle thing, and that softness—fluid, adaptable, decentralized—is far harder to extinguish than steel.

True to water's ways, staying present with our hurt parts is the medicine here, allowing our feelings to seep through our bones, surrendering with presence to the ride that suffering may demand of us, so as to let flow through us the traumas that need healing at this delicate time. And to those inclined, as Willis recommends in her article, the process can be enhanced by forms of ritual to grieve, speak, and release old wounds back to the earth, for composting and renewal.

What you search for is sleeping in your very being.
And that which sleeps and dreams of sweet water
is the taste of the divine in you.
The true way is who and where you already are.
~ Rumi

5

Make of Thyself a Light: Leo

~ July 23-August 22

Sunflower bursts forth unbidden from a terrace pot

Even after all this time
The sun never says to the earth,
'You owe me.'
Look what happens
With a love like that,
It lights up the whole sky.
~ Hafiz

The Leo archetype, ruled by the Sun, in its highest essence partakes of the light that makes all life possible in its great generosity. The Sun fuels life on Earth, and as such symbolically sparks our hearts with the love that holds the universe together. The Buddha's dying words to his chief disciple, Ananda, were to "take thyself for a light," because when we do so, we ourselves become a burning sun, a light both for ourselves and for others.

As the next Fixed sign after Taurus, Leo is concerned with that which is of *value*—as Fixed energy wants to preserve the capacity for life on Earth. And for Leo, a Fire sign, the value is felt in what shines through its personhood—ultimately through the heart—rather than life's comforts and securities, gifts and pleasures, which are earthy Taurus' realm.

And as the Sun is to life on Earth, so too is the heart to we humans, both physically and emotionally—the beating heart of course being what keeps us physically alive, as well as the symbolic center of our love. As the Sun nourishes the leaves, whose chlorophyll absorbs its life-giving light, so the heart sends life-giving chi nourishment through the blood—this an energy healer recently advised me of, having recently had some heart-related symptoms in the wake of Long Covid.

The healer had already given me an effective protocol of supplements and teas to address my symptoms of exhaustion, brain fog, and headaches, but some heart symptoms were persisting. Checking me out with her energy medicine techniques, she determined that I didn't need to change anything outward, but simply engage with the unusual practice of circulating light through my blood. As soon as I tried it, I felt a calming, like something falling into place. She advised that I let the light radiate into the networks of my body, which is exactly what the Leo archetype does—radiate its light into its networks!

And too, at this time of late summer, here in the north the sun's light radiates with a diffuse shade of gold, in tune with the glittering gold linked with Sun-ruled Leo. Archetypally we now meet the Lion King, signifying the glory of a heart-centered, generous and charismatic leader.

Considering the politics of our time, we may be rolling our eyes at the antiquated notion, thinking, *in your dreams, a generous and charismatic leader!* But dream we must as, despite the off-centered Leo display—writ larger day by day—of prideful attachment to largesse and self-adulation that we're seeing from a certain orange-headed wannabe king with Leo rising, the archetypal call to this sign's higher gifts of self-confidence and self-respect is here for us to heed. For when centered, Leo's capacity to hold authority with inspired creativity and warmth serves as a beacon for others.

Center stage

Understandably our attention may now be trained on the abundant abuses being imposed on the peoples of the world—signified by the Aquarius archetype—particularly those being marginalized, detained, deported, and killed. And yet Leo, the sign of the empowered self, remains an important energy to embrace, as polarity partner to Aquarius. As significators of the Individual and the Group, Leo and Aquarius need each other to function optimally.

In addition to the leader, Leo is associated with the entertainer, the one who infuses their joyful glow from whatever size stage they beam from. Conjuring up the image of Leo on a *large* stage, it's interesting to consider that shining star Taylor Swift has her South Node—what she specialized in childhood and prior lives—in Leo. She was built for the limelight!

Proud peacock struts amidst the lime lights, Filoli Gardens, Woodside, CA

Most of us are not so called—yet Leo nudges us to ask ourselves: how are we radiating what we love, and what turns us on, in our lives? Or how might we do so in the future? It is important to make space to tune into this notion, of centering ourselves in giving and the joy it engenders, particularly as potent counterforce to the notes of discord, outrage, and fear that abound in our time.

Oddly, the car radio during these summer days has been blasting the golden oldies of youth, invoking the carefree 'summer groove' of times gone by. While it's a strange disconnect, this is our task: to connect who we were with who we are becoming and *have yet* to become, to forge this union of our past and future parts, metabolizing our real (and feared) losses, and facing forward with Leonine *coeur*-age (*coeur* meaning heart in French).

Joining our reflections of the past with the celebratory fires of the present is in resonance with the archetypal impulses of our two bright 'luminaries,' Moon and Sun, back-to-back rulers of the summer month signs Cancer and Leo. Moon-ruled Cancer—introspective, yin energy concerned with family, emotional security, and the past—segues to dramatic Leo, with its outward-thrusting, yang creative force, shining its "I Am" light.

Love and ice cream

In step with this, I've been surfing the memory drift of summers past—especially those of my early years spent on remote Nantucket Island (New England's mystical counterpart to Scotland's Hebrides Isles). Of course, modern day Nantucket has greatly changed, but it was still untrammeled by modernity until the early 90s when SUVs hit the scene. There was a time-out-of-time quality to my early experiences there, which rendered in me a deep, true love of the land in her many manifestations and moods. This to me is part of what 'summer love' has always been about.

Into this reverie of mine, Canadian singer-songwriter Sarah McLaughlin's sweet song from the 80s, "Ice Cream," popped up on my phone the other day, looping in my head for days thereafter. Of course, ice cream figured centrally into the Nantucket experience, as one of summer's essential delights. But the melodious song goes further, centering around the lyric, *Your love is better than ice cream.*

This invokes a dream my ex-husband had decades ago, in the earlier years of attending our Sufi meditation group, where dreams were shared and discussed for hours. Details escape, but in the dream he was serving up ice cream to folks at a stand. Arriving at an understanding of the dream, the revelation came, *Ice cream is something everybody loves!* And indeed, everybody loved Jenya! One of our Sufi friends dubbed him "a heart with legs!"

A pair of eyebrow-raising synchronicities with the ice cream theme ensued, one while watching a Steven Colbert monologue that included a Sarah McLaughlin song from the same album as "Ice Cream" in a spoofy farewell tribute to "Kamala's 'brat' summer." This right after Biden informed the country of his withdrawal from the presidential race, and the news outlets (including Colbert) were abuzz about how ice cream was served afterwards in the Rose Garden to hundreds of White House staffers. (*Post mortem*: fast forward two years, and the Rose Garden, like much but not all, of paradise, has been paved over.)

The creative imperative

But moving on to more serious Leo stuff than ice cream—even though everyone loves it—I came across a potent piece online in *The Marginalian*, exploring Mary Oliver's thoughts on how to make time for creativity amidst all of life's distractions[28] (something I can surely relate to!). With the Sun as life's very creator, it follows that the Leo archetype bestows on us our own personal forms of creativity. Oliver points to the fact that it is not just worldly distractions that keep us from our creative work, but we ourselves. She observes:

"…that the self can interrupt the self—and does is a darker and more curious matter." She then describes what she sees as three selves within: the childhood self, "which we spend our lives trying to weave into the continuity of our personal identity;" an adult "servant of the hours, who is slave to To Dos"; and a third self, "occasional in some of us, tyrant in others. This self is out of love with the ordinary; it is out of love with time. It has a hunger for eternity." She elucidates:

Extraordinary Zowie zinnia

Intellectual work sometimes, spiritual work certainly, artistic work always—these are forces that fall within [the creative life's] grasp, forces that must travel beyond the realm of the hour and the restraint of the habit. Nor can the actual work be well separated from the entire life. Like the knights of the Middle Ages, there is little the creatively inclined person can do but prepare himself, body and spirit, for the labor to come—for his adventures are all unknown. In truth, the work itself is the adventure. And no artist could go about this work, or would want to, with less than extraordinary energy and concentration. The extraordinary is what art is about.

It is said that art, in whatever form, is what can and will save us, at levels both great and small, even though it is no longer supported in our public schools as comprehensively as it once was. So it's by hook or crook (there's a creative expression!) that we have to nourish and support our creative genius, and that of our progeny, and ask ourselves what creative contribution can we yet make in service to life? What spark can we cultivate and offer, in whatever way, shape, or form, however small, simple, and local? All voices, scribbles, and seeds are welcome as the waters of change threaten to become rougher.

Fruits of passion: our children

Love, passion, and their progeny, creativity, are the trinity of the Leo essence, and joy is the by-product that fountains up through it. So whether it's x meets y, and their shared passion produces a child, or you are an artist of some sort—including an artist of Life—creative acts draw inspiration from the passion of the heart and, in turn, the inspiration to share the wealth from which they're sourced.

Without love and passion, we wouldn't be running around putting up decorations, performing puppet shows with hand-felted puppets, crafting gem-laden paper crowns, and baking special cakes to celebrate our loved ones, such as our beloved children or grandchildren. My daughter happens to be a Leo Sun sign, and her dad and I did all of the above and then some to honor her birthdays! (But once she discovered store-bought *ice cream* cakes, my 'special cakes' were nixed. Just as well—baking *not* my creative gift!)

Of course, our creative acts can also celebrate the beauty of the earth, in the form of our gardens, paintings, poetry, music and film—the sky's the limit. But given that Leo, per se, is an archetype of the radiant self, the delightful innocence and playful self-expression of children very much sync with this archetype.

Considering our harvest

In the Celtic cultures, August 1 marks the cross-quarter point midway between summer solstice and fall equinox, signaling the beginning of fall and of the harvest. August is thus a month of celebration and gratitude for the fruits of a season of creative work, from both humans, and Gaia herself—a time for harvest fairs and festivals that honor the dedication of farmers, bakers, and artisans alike.

This weekend I will be volunteering at my local Gravenstein Apple Fair, which honors what once was the native pride and joy of Sonoma County, the Gravenstein apple, but which has been sidelined by the proliferation of more lucrative vineyards in recent decades.

Thankfully we do still honor the humble apple with this event, at which I recall my daughter won a goldfish at one of its games, over 20 years ago—with gold being our Leo theme!

Called *Lammas* in Scotland, and *Lughnasadh* in Ireland, this Celtic festival has been traditionally celebrated by baking bread from the season's first wheat. These days bread, and the grain it comes from, are something most of us pick up at the store, but in ancient times, grain was sacred—of central importance to survival—and so associated with the wheel of life and death.

With the harvest in mind, we might be asking ourselves: What is our own personal harvest from this point in the year? Or, extending time: What am I seeking to harvest in this next season of my life? This could be garden gleanings, creative undertakings, or perhaps the delights of our progeny, as well as romance, all being significators of the 5th House in the zodiac, naturally ruled by Leo.

Flower harvest of the hour, including Lion's tail (Leonotus leonoris), bottom left, and to right

The Greek goddess Demeter and her daughter Persephone, mentioned in the Cancer chapter in connection with the Eleusinian Mysteries of death and rebirth, are also significant here at the time of *Lammas*. Given that the grain was connected with Life in ancient times (no gluten free diets then!), Demeter, goddess of agriculture, presided over both grain and the harvest. Her presence (and this festival) therefore invokes the notion of gratitude and celebration for the blessings of the earth, and the 'death' phase at hand along the seasonal wheel. (*Demeter sadly walks the land, the dying grasses in her hand* were the lyrics of an old pagan round I've sung since my 20s.)

Changing light

Whether sad or exciting, August is the month when we in the northern climes feel the first whispers of fall—through the early leaf color turnings, the sudden cool breeze, or a special slant of light—invoking perhaps a cherishing of these closing weeks under the Sun's bright domain.

I first noticed the unique quality of diffuse August light decades ago, walking in the early evening across the dry golden hillsides of my remote west Sonoma County homeland, calling in a recognition of something both special and fleeting. Out walking the other day, I again sensed this unique vibration of light arising, with the words *"light in August"* coming to me, from the title of the book by William Faulkner. Online I found an excerpt of his about this light:

> . . . *in August in Mississippi there's a few days somewhere about the middle of the month when suddenly there's a foretaste of fall, it's cool, there's a lambency, a soft, luminous quality to the light, as though it came not from just today but from back in the old classic times. It might have fauns and satyrs and the gods and—from Greece, from Olympus in it somewhere. It lasts just for a day or two, then it's gone…[it invokes] a luminosity older than our Christian civilization.*

I do sense a sort of ancient luminosity in this waning August light. Yet, it can also still be deadly hot. Housebound for some of these steamy days, doors and windows shut to the heat outside, I can lose touch with the natural world, barely hearing the treasures of the wind's shimmer through the leaves, or the birds' news, save the penetrating soft coo of mourning doves. I can still take delight, however, in the sight of my prize volunteer sunflower—especially as flowers (the earth's creative gold medalists), and particularly *sunflowers*, are a Leo symbol!

The heart as master connector

I recently happened to pull down a book that's been on my shelf for 10 years, inherited from my ex-husband, who passed away that many years ago. *The Secret Teachings of Plants* is by Stephen Buhner, respected plant medicine researcher and author of numerous impactful books. Perusing the chapters for the first time, I was stunned to discover that the whole book was in fact about the heart. This while preparing my class on Leo. Indeed, the subtitle, which I had not initially noted, is *The Intelligence of the Heart in the Direct Perception of Nature.* (Can't make this stuff up, as they say.)

Endowed with a poetic spirit, Buhner generously (as Leo energy does) sprinkles the book with quotes from Kabir, Henry David Thoreau, Goethe, and Luther Burbank, tying together the physical and the spiritual all in the name of the powerful and truly magnificent heart. He points to its capacity to hook us directly into the communications of the natural world—particularly plants—but rocks and other life forms as well. In a powerful passage he relates his first deep contact with wild nature, after high school, 12,000 feet high in the mountains.

Cosmos seedling has a heart

...slowly, my heart began beating with the rhythms of the glade, my tiny life held in the embrace of its older and more powerful waves. And those waves were a language, carrying within them a meaning far older than words, telling me of being wanted, a part of something that would always be. Murmuring that in this place was my place, in this heart my heart. But deeper still, under all of that, there was a substance, some soul food that I needed to become human, that came to me now. I breathed it in with every breath, took it in with every heartbeat. A food as important to my spirit as my mother's milk had been to my body. And something in me opened up, some tiny doorway within me, and through it flowed this substance. From me, too, it flowed, and the glade took it in and rejoiced. And in that moment, I bonded with the world...[29]

Buhner was influenced by author Joseph Chilton Pearce's pioneering discovery that the heart functions as a powerful 'brain' in the human body, with the two operating together as a "heart-mind matrix." Pearce writes in his book, *The Biology of Transcendence,*

In an efficient biological unfolding, the intelligence of our heart and the intellect in our head should function as an interdependent dynamic, each influencing and giving rise to the other. The breakdown or impairment of this reciprocal action is brought about by its cultural counterfeits of myth and religion. This, in turn, brings about both our fundamental split of self and our self-wrought woes—providing an explanation for why it is that we build bombs with one hand even as we gesture toward peace and love with the other.[30]

While I take issue with his suggestion that myth, like religion, is a 'cultural counterfeit', I appreciate that Buhner describes how the "heart-based cognition" of Indigenous peoples the world over and throughout history is what enables them to listen to and understand directly from plants themselves what their medicinal uses are. He also writes in detail about the hugely powerful electromagnetic fields of the heart, which extend in 3D around the body in a *torus*, a semi-spherical fractal that flows continually through space.

Measured with magnetic field meters, the electromagnetic field that the heart produces is some five thousand times more powerful than that created by the brain. While strongest at the body's surface, it extends out further than human measuring devices can detect.[31]

He invites us to focus outside ourselves and attend to the energetic encounters we can feel with persons, plants, and rocks, stating that when we do so, we feel a range of emotional impressions based on those organisms' electromagnetic fields, and how these alter our own.

This is, in fact, the source of the deep feelings that come from our immersion in wild landscapes…And these externally generated feelings are an important and essential source of emotions for all human beings, for we emerged not only from our mothers' wombs, but also from the wildness of the world. We developed nestled not only in our mothers' electromagnetic fields, but also within the larger electromagnetic field of the Earth.[32]

The King must die

Throughout time, the regal Leo archetype has been associated with king- and queenliness, the likes of which include the potent myths of Olympian Greek god Zeus, the lion Aslan in C.S. Lewis' *The Lion, the Witch, and the Wardrobe*, and King Arthur, leader of the Knights of the Round Table, and seeker after the Holy Grail. In ancient times, the Egyptian Queen of Sheba was considered the daughter of the Sun, her lineage emanating from the Ethiopian "King of kings," *Jah*—with *Jah* being the god of the Rastafarians in Ethiopia and Jamaica.

Yet in many respects ours is a time of moving out of the king-focused era (witness the failed health of King Charles, stricken so soon after he assumed the throne), and into the pulse of the Aquarian archetype—concerned with the big picture view of life, the future, and the collective. We are transitioning from the Age of Pisces into that of Aquarius, and emphasizing this, Pluto, planet of death and transformation, is now in this sign until the mid-2040s.

Sunflower lights: the one and the many

Here in the flux of the death-rebirth cycle, we are witnessing the dying of an aged-out era, of the ailing Piscean "Grail King," and as well, the puerile manifestations of a young, off-centered Aquarius archetype: autocracy by sociopaths, dark takeover schemes by the 'technocrats' with their disembodied, heartless AI, and visions of occupying outer space. Astrologers suggest this is to purge the shadowy, Aquarian detritus out of humanity's system, before the more beautiful manifestations of the sign—founded on a vision that honors all life in its diversity, with the needs, limits, and gifts of the earth front and center—can take root. We cannot know the outcome, of course, but I feel it serves us all to hold and live into this greater vision.

The legend of the Grail King (like the Age of Pisces) is associated with Christ as individual savior, but in addition to its affiliation with Pisces, the fishes (with *The Fisher King* being a common designation for this mythical king), the story speaks to the Leo archetype, that of the blazing Sun, who rules from the throne. Marie-Louise von Franz and Emma Jung, in *The Grail Legend,* discuss the king archetype, quoting Carl Jung:

> *Among primitives, the King, especially in his original role as chief of the tribe, represents in his own person the centre [sic] of the life of the people. In him the divine "spirit" of the tribe is incarnated, on him depend the psychic and physical welfare of the people, even to the rain and the fruitfulness of fields and livestock. Psychologically he represents a symbol of the Self become visible in a human being, to which the entire social and psychic organization of his people is adjusted.*[33]

Von Franz and E. Jung go on to point out, however, that in primitive cultures the king was ritually killed off when showing signs of old age or illness, so that the tribal spirit could live on through a more competent successor. They cite experts who suggest that the ailing Grail King is a symbol of a "stricken society," or "mankind in a fallen state."

The work of our time: Leo-Aquarius synthesis

In his online webinar, "Astrology for Times of Upheaval," depth psychological astrologer Laurence Hillman (son of famed depth psychologist James Hillman) suggests that the integration of the Leo-Aquarius polarity is the most important task of our time. With innovator Uranus being the modern ruler of Aquarius, we are beckoned to an expanding consciousness; yet we cannot deny the importance of the centered self, the Leo project. What is needed is a serious 'uplevel' of this archetype of the individual, such that it returns to its noble roots, and casts out the arrogance and self-preoccupation that has crept into the psyche of the era.

Leo benefits from remembering the Aquarian 'big picture', and the community of all beings, and not just the shining of its own bright light. And Aquarius needs Leo's heart-centered charisma to lend it the confidence to step out from the recesses of the crowd and take a passionate stand so that it's not stuck in the isolated, disconnected wings. Leo brings fun, too!

Aquarius specializes in innovative visions and high-minded missions, but can lose sight of caring about the particulars, including individuals! (A highly innovative Aquarian friend from decades ago, living in an isolated setting, once quipped, "Friends are over-rated!") This is why we need heart-centered, generous Leo, to keep us focused at the level of our humanity, even while our systems are shaking down, or up.

Love lights shining: alstromaria lily and rose campion

Kosmos Journal recently published an article that voices a uniquely Aquarian vision of leadership, of a cohesive future that operates through anarchy, relying on *resonance* as the "leader of leaderlessness." Author Arabella Thais suggests,

In an anarchic society, the leader is not the one with the most control, but the one with the most alignment—the one who is so attuned to the deeper frequency of the Real that others orient around them effortlessly, not out of obedience but recognition…This is how the cosmos leads. Not with domination—but through radiance.

[...] This is what I call impulsional sovereignty—a mode of being in which one's actions arise not from external commands, but from interior concordance with the Whole. In mystical Christianity, this is agape; in Taoism, it is the Tao; in Jung, it is individuation: the harmony of the Self with the archetypal totality.[34]

Thais references agape, the highest form of love and charity, as the source of the cohering 'radiance' of which she speaks. To me this offers an exciting possibility for a 'high frequency' Leo-Aquarius synthesis.

6

GODDESS IN THE DETAILS: VIRGO

~ August 23-September 22

Wheat, in her perfect order, Snape Maltings, Suffolk, UK

Amazing how quickly summer flies, even while it can seem eternal in those deep Cancerian moments with the water and the light, or steeped in the rush of the heart that Leo brings on, whether through celebration, creativity, or Earth love. But, with the fall equinox fast approaching, we now find ourselves back in the saddle of common things, earth-bound and focused, ready to apply ourselves to the hard work of mending and tending to the fabric of life. To be sure, Virgo's archetypal filter, through which the Sun at this time casts its rays, is trained on the ordinary, on the harvesting of the fruits of the earth (bountiful during Virgo season) and the careful work of separating the chaff from the wheat.

A practical Earth sign, Virgo's call is to compensate for Leo's exuberant showings at a time of year when culturally we buckle down and submit to the routines of school and work. As a Virgo Sun sign myself, I must say that as much as I am at times deeply entranced by the drift of summer, I often feel at sea in these months (not just literally!). For introverted Virgo, home base is about being productive, ordered and useful, and as a mutable sign, it prefers to work within a regular routine of sorts. This is our fun! So when the colors of fall start to reveal their lights, as did my little Japanese maple last week, a cheer arises from the heart.

Down to Earth

I talked in the Leo chapter of how in the Celtic calendar, the Greek goddess Demeter is associated with the August 1 cross-quarter festival of *Lammas*, linking August to the harvest, which this festival initiates. But in the Gregorian calendar, September—and Virgo—as well heralds the harvest. Indeed, the harvest is a two-month affair, starting with wheat, and culminating with the fruits.

Stepping back from Leo's lavish pageantry, honing in on what Virgo says *really* matters, is a bit like what Monday feels like after the weekend. Some may groan, but perhaps Moon-day is not all bad. As the only sign whose associated image is a person— the maiden, Virgo is intrinsically linked to the virgin goddess of the Moon, Artemis, as well as the Egyptian goddess Isis, overseer of agriculture and healing practices. Like the Virgo maiden, Isis was depicted carrying a sheaf of wheat; and in an ancient cosmology tale it has it that she dropped the sheaf, after which it rose to the sky and became the Milky Way.

One could say that returning to Moon-day, after spirit-ual 'Sun-Day', with the energetic shift from Sun-ruled Leo to another Moon-affiliated sign (like Cancer), Virgo, we are called 'down to earth,' to the practical, feminine, imminent matters–those of tending the material incarnations of spirit in the everyday tasks—all of which is Virgo's business, and joy!

Good Medicine

Given the archetype's association with ancient healing practices, it follows that in modern times, Virgo energy is often preoccupied with alternative health, herbs, and nutrition. Was I surprised then, when, once tucked in to Virgo season, I saw the announcement that a musical group coming to my local community center bore the name, *The Vitamin Quartet*? Further investigation found that this quartet was featured in the hit Netflix series, *Bridgerton*, which I consumed quite happily. I tell you, these archetypes have their sneaky ways of showing up in our lives, if we know what to look for.

Issuing from those early times of separating wheat from chaff, Virgo provides us with the ever-important gift of discernment, as well as the impulse towards ordering and perfecting. Purifying, addressing inefficiencies, sorting…these are her jam! But most folks aren't so built, and too much of this staying on top of things can get one into trouble relationally, which is why Virgo has traditionally been one of the most maligned signs. Virgo energy does tend to 'sweat the small stuff,' and is known to cast a spell of fuss and worry around the minutia (like diet and health routines) that others could care less about. It can obsess about what needs fixing, what 'makes sense,' or what could go wrong. But without Virgo, the cogs in the gears of life would falter, and the big Fire sign visions would not be made manifest. We need this energy!

In the years during and after Covid, and with the negative effects of vaccinations on some (including myself), many have faced issues with energy, mental clarity, sleep, inflammatory pain, and heart function. Also, there's aging. It's a fact that the microbiomes in our bodies are changing in these very changing times. We may be forced to slow down, tend and befriend our bodies in new and concerted ways, and drink in the simple beauties around us.

Healing garden time—breathing with the devas

One method for addressing the physiological effects of stress and negative emotions is breathwork. As a trained facilitator of Mind Body Skills, of which mindful breathing is a core tenet, I have personally experienced how breathwork transmutes anxiety, whether on the MRI table, or navigating amidst crazed highway drivers. It's also been medically proven that deep diaphragmatic breathing, with a long exhale, activates the parasympathetic nervous system and calms the 'fight or flight' response. Revered Buddhist teacher, Thich Nhat Hanh, suggests in his book, *Being Peace*, that we breathe in stating, *I am calm,* and breath out smiling.

Breathwork is high octane Virgo medicine, as Virgo can be prone to edgy nerves. Even when hard at work (as Virgo often is), taking conscious breath breaks mitigates the adrenaline-driven 'get it done' mode, returning one to the gentle sea of body awareness. We can strengthen the effect by taking nerve-calming herbs like chamomile or St. Johnswort, as well as invoking English Saint Julian of Norwich (1343-1416), who said, famously, "All shall be well, all shall be well, and all manner of things shall be well." My Russian-born husband used a similar phrase, "Everything will be okay" (phonetically: *fsyaw bood-yeht har-o-sho*), which was the first Russian phrase I learned in our rustic, back-to-the-land life together. I needed it!

Virgo antidote: *it's all good*

Personally, I've been working on reforming my Virgo lens on life, adding a healthy dose of Jupiterian/Sagittarius buoyancy and gratitude to my diet. In these rapidly changing times of ours, I believe focusing on what's good is a key to the way forward, and through, whatever may come.

Virgo knows that in order to improve things (what editors get hired for!), one has to eliminate flaws and imperfections. Virgo excels at detecting patterns and establishing viable systems, all in the name of efficiency. While useful in the workplace, trained on other realms, this mindset (which could be you in some part of your chart, don't forget) can be prone to seeing the glass half-empty. (Half-full is traditionally Sagittarius's realm, who, with perhaps some coaching from Gemini, coined the phrase, *It's all good,* which of course to Virgo is delusional folly.)

So while Virgo energy is often tuned towards functionality, it can get derailed by its 'what's missing' orientation. As well, Mercury-ruled Virgo, hard at the work of discrimination and discernment, has trouble feeling and expressing emotions, and is thereby mentally 'top-heavy.' Given that what's in our minds affects our health, Virgo is known to somatize emotions, thereby bypassing them, and instead spending much attention on migrating and mysterious ailments—sometimes ongoingly, sometimes at key transformational junctures.

Bruce Lipton, author of *The Biology of Belief*, reminds us that we have a choice about giving space to negative thoughts. Brain chemistry, he states, is a translation of our beliefs, with negative beliefs walling us off from health. He suggests that we take on the challenge of priming the brain to change its circuitry, by slipping in new beliefs, behaviors, and outcomes that diverge from those founded in the past.

Inventing the world we see through a tilt of the lens

Taming the beasty mind

At her wisest, Mercury-informed Virgo works with the power of words, of how they're used as frames, and of the yarns they spin. These determine our reality. In this vein, I think of the book, *The Course in Miracles Experiment*, by Pam Grout, which talks of how one can change one's life by rewiring the mind. This is great Virgo medicine, good for any who specialize in negative or fear-based thinking (this can be Virgo's polarity friend, Pisces, on a bad day, too!). She writes,

The quantum field is an infinite mashup of possibilities. It contains countless waves, dancing around in countless states, countless positions, countless possibilities. Each has its own energy and frequency. It isn't until the waves are measured—or chosen— that they coalesce into one material reality, thus destroying the original configuration where "all is possible." Once we decide that, say, "life's a struggle," or that "people always disappoint me," we collapse that wave and lose touch with all the rest. [CIM] explains that I have invented the world I see. So do I want to continue inventing a world out of my complaints?

The material world as it's currently configured is based on fear. It's based on the belief that everything is out to get us: our politicians, our food, our bodies…other countries… Every news report, commission, political speech, and self-help book is based on our unending fascination with "what's wrong."

As no doubt we've heard, what we focus on with our mind, we attract. In New Age circles, this has been dubbed the 'Law of Attraction,' and is too often used for self-serving ends. But there is a beautiful truth herein, which addresses Virgo's angsty mental tilt. To grow the transformations we seek in our life, we benefit from adding a splash of Sagittarian uplift to our morning (and midday!) brew—whatever that may look like (but likely *not* the news headlines!).

Perhaps it's reading an inspiring poem, or stepping outside to imbibe the fresh morning air, the birdsong, the early sun's rays. Perhaps it's tuning in to the calming, unitive breath as it moves into our body—maybe with movements and stretches—or connecting to the signature of the day through the elements, or seasons. Regardless of how we get there, it's helpful to find a sense of peace in the body-mind, to shift the mental frown by remembering ourselves back into the greater whole, and finding patience and trust in the way life unfolds.

Why Then Do We Not Despair

Everything is plundered, betrayed, sold,
Death's great black wing scrapes the air,
Misery gnaws to the bone.
Why then do we not despair?

By day, from the surrounding woods,
cherries blow summer into town;
at night the deep transparent skies
glitter with new galaxies.

And the miraculous comes so close
to the ruined, dirty houses—
something not known to anyone at all,
but wild in our breast for centuries.
- Anna Akhmatova

Balance of Light and Dark

September is a month of ever shortening of days, as we approach the equinox at Libra's ingress. Relevant here is that Virgo, like Cancer, is affiliated with the myth of the Greek goddess Persephone, whose fate it is to spend half her life in the Underworld dark, and half above-ground, filled with the delights of flowers and fields. This love of Earth along with the turn towards the darkness is, I think, inherent to the Virgo spirit, and the Akhmatova poem above reflects Virgo's capacity for being 'swept away' by the miraculous beauty of cherries and woods, despite the plethora of despairs. Independent and introspective, Virgo welcomes a modicum of withdrawal to process and dwell in life's complexities. (All this splashing around in sunshine and light gets a bit much, she says wryly.)

Light meets dark in the Scottish Highlands

In its inward phases, however, the Virgo mentality can fall into dwelling on guilt or shame for failing to reach the high standards set for itself. It's a paradox, for while Virgo's is the realm of 'common things', it longs to see its ideals, seeded by polarity partner Pisces, made manifest. Falling short of this, Virgo becomes her own worst critic. In such times, engaging with ordinary tasks—cleaning, gardening, cooking, or fixing things—helps to recenter and ground.

I once had a potent dream that pointed to this truth. I was walking along a wide beach towards the sea, keen on merging into the inviting waters when, blocking my trajectory, I encountered a deep hole dug in the sand, inside of which rested a giant spool of thread. The message I gleaned was that I need to tend to the mundane, symbolized by household mending, before uniting with the sea of Oneness. While imbued with devotion and longing for the divine, Virgo's role is to remain in practical service to life.

Longing and humility

This brings us to humility, another Virgo quality that counterbalances Leonine pride. Humility was considered by another honored, early female saint to be the greatest of all virtues. Hildegard von Bingen—12 C. visionary, composer, and healer—wrote extensively about herbs and nutrition, and composed the world's first opera, *Ordo Virtutum*, which depicts the 35 virtues within. The title of one of her many songs, *O viridissima virga*, translates as "Hail, oh greenest branch," affirming the link between Virgo/virgin with the natural world's greenness, freshness, and innocence—qualities dear to Hildegard's heart. Humility was Hildegard's 'supreme virtue', as it demanded acceptance that the connection to the Divine exists beyond human understanding. To know it, one must follow one's 'true nature.'

There is a Sufi saying that speaks to the Virgoan desire to serve: *I do not ask to see, I do not ask to know, I ask only to be used.* A third great saint to invoke for this archetype, Mother Teresa, had Sun, Mercury, and Mars all in Virgo. In her collected letters we learn that, while she had one powerful vision of being wed to Christ at the age of 18, she sustained herself for the rest of her life of tireless service purely on devotion, with no more affirming visions.

Humility also includes the concept that, no matter what we may know or excel at, there's always more to learn. This gets at the heart of another aspect of the Virgo mindset—that one's body of knowledge or level of expertise is never complete—this explains why Virgo is dubbed "the scholar of the zodiac." One can always be, and do, better! While perhaps exhausting at times, this attitude surely keeps life interesting, with ever-widening frontiers of knowledge and wisdom to explore.

Being a mutable sign is one factor explaining Virgo's love of learning, growth, and change. For Virgo in particular these endeavors require periods of retreat—for reflection and metabolizing all that has been absorbed from her experiences and exchanges, whether conscious or unconscious. In terms of the wheel of the Zodiac, Virgo's role is great: that of reconciling all that has come before in the first five signs towards building a self.

Aries was about arrival—*here I am;* Taurus, about getting secure with food and a roof, and creature comforts; Gemini extends outwards through learning and communicating; Cancer finds emotional security and belonging from mother, family, and home; and Leo rejoices in its creative accomplishments—ROAR!

Magnolia flower, Sonoma Botanical Gardens, Kenwood, CA

Now, before moving on to the second half of the 12 zodiacal signs, where we begin the journey of relatedness to others with Libra, we have Virgo, who seeks to temper and integrate all that has come until now. Consider an electrical transformer, which has to 'step down' and coalesce the power coming from a transmission station in order for it to be safe, functional, and practically used in buildings and homes, and you have Virgo!

God in a hazel nut

It's actually quite a job, which is why Virgo is one of the most complex signs. Virgo needs to connect deeper than the conditioned ego manifestation—what it puts out into the world—and does so through both communion with the more-than-human worlds, and examining its mental frameworks, and shadows, so as to connect to the divine spark of authenticity. For some, this requires receiving the Light and integrating it within one's being, often in a hidden way. The life of anchoress Julian of Norwich exemplifies this theme.

When Julian was 30-years-old and on the brink of death from a serious illness, she experienced 16 visions (which she called 'showings'). Hearing Jesus speaking to her for several hours, she had a revelation of 'unitive consciousness,' after which she felt compelled to remove herself from ordinary life in order to reflect on her profound experience. She asked the bishop at St. Julian's Church in Norwich, England to build a hermit's enclosure for her, where she spent the next 20 years in contemplation and prayer, seeking true understanding of her visions.

Eventually, she wrote *Revelations of Divine Love*, about these 'showings.' Here is an excerpt:

> *And in this he showed me a little thing, the quantity of a hazel nut, lying in the palm of my hand, as it seemed. And it was as round as any ball. I looked upon it with the eye of my understanding, and thought, 'What may this be?' And it was answered generally thus, 'It is all that is made.' I marveled how it might last, for I thought it might suddenly have fallen to nothing for littleness. And I was answered in my understanding: It lasts and ever shall, for God loves it. And so have all things their beginning by the love of God.*
>
> *In this little thing I saw three properties. The first is that God made it. The second, that God loves it. And the third, that God keeps it.*

Retreat and receive

The Divine light penetrates through all creation, from great to small. And while the daily round of serviceful operations is Virgo's 'in life' role, Virgo's periodic, and essential, retreat phases help with the never-ending undertaking of refinement—where she undergoes an interior, creative process of transformation, of sifting and winnowing, so as to discern the way forward. For Virgo is a type of gate-keeper, gifted at preparing for her next 'version' of earthly service.

It can be at times a delicate ground to tread, sorting through one's responses and thoughts about others and the world, navigating between owning one's projections (e.g., the blame we've cast on others), claiming self-responsibility where it is due, yet being careful not to get mired in self-deprecation or self-doubt. For while Virgo is known for its critical nature, the greatest object of critique is herself. (Apologies to male readers—I use 'she', as her totem is the maiden.)

Dandelion foot bitters brewing

Bitter Medicine

The shared challenge of polarity partners Virgo and Pisces is to both listen for and hold the awareness of perfection without getting caught in despair over the fact that the Ideal as imagined cannot be landed here on earth. We need Virgo's humility to accept and submit to the sometimes not so sexy, but organic 'humus' that is earthly life.

Not exactly *a propos* of sex (!), Virgo has associations to the Virgin Mary. In Hebrew the root *mr* means "bitter"—fitting, because Virgo, while a loving nurturer of beings, treads a somewhat bitter path, plagued with anxiety in the 'self-purification' endeavor. Astrologer Mark Jones refers to Virgo as an archetype of 'crisis,' as its process of refinement does indeed involve a type of alchemical 'cooking,' to which one doesn't always respond gracefully! To ease a challenged Virgo heart, good medicine is found in invoking feelings of connectedness to a transcendent oneness, which is the gift of Pisces.

The late musician Leonard Cohen, with Virgo Sun and Pisces Moon, struggled at times with depression and loneliness. As shared from his autobiography, *I'm Your Man*, by depth psychological astrologer Safron Rossi in an online webinar[35], Cohen writes poignantly of how the Spanish poet Federico Garcia Lorca helped him find 'big picture' (Pisces) solace in his personal mental health struggles.

> 'The universe [Lorca] revealed seemed very familiar,' his words illuminating 'a landscape that you thought you alone walked on.' Part of that landscape was loneliness. 'When something was said in a certain kind of way, it seemed to embrace the cosmos. It's not just my heart, but every heart was involved, and the loneliness dissolved, and you felt that you were this aching creature in the midst of an aching cosmos, and the ache was okay. Not only was it okay, but it was the way you embraced the Sun and the Moon.'

This 'embrace of Sun and Moon' is in fact part of Virgo's work—the integration of the blazing Leonine Sun essence, with the shadowy, internal realms of the feminine Moon nature. Here perhaps we can understand the 'virginal' nature of Virgo. Associated with the goddess Hestia's Vestal Virgins, Virgo is not necessarily always chaste, but rather instinctively lord (or lady) over and unto herself—not in need of a marriage partner or male counterpart to complete her, or give her direction, as she is set to the work of the alchemical 'sacred marriage' between Sun and Moon, with which Libra will continue on.

7)

KEEPING BEAUTY IN MIND:
LIBRA

~ September 23-August 22

When the Celtic Imagination searched for the structures of shelter and meaning,
it raised its eyes to the mountains and the heavens, and put its trust in
the faithful patterns of the Sun, the stars, the Moon, and the seasons.

Long before then the Greek imagination had raised its eye to the heavens also,
and seen in the Cosmos a beautiful order, which was to become the heart of their
notion of Beauty. The Cosmos, in its order and pattern and rhythm, was beautiful.

So all the uncertainty and the confusion of life could somehow be endured, because
they were happening within a pattern of Order and Beauty. This Beauty presided over
the journey between Awakening and Surrender, awakening each day to view first the
Source and then the Horizon, the Invisible and the Visible.[36]
~John O'Donohue

Ushering in the season change at the fall equinox, the ingress of Libra signals a significant moment in the zodiacal round—Libra being one of the four cardinal signs that initiates a new quarter or phase. The other cardinal signs include Aries, kicking off the spring equinox; Cancer, ushering in the summer solstice; and after Libra, Capricorn, the winter solstice. On the zodiacal wheel, connecting each of these four signs' ingress (entrance) points traces a cross through the circle, giving them particular significance among the archetypes.

Polar opposites Aries and Libra connect the horizontal axis of the cross, signifying self vs. other, while Cancer and Capricorn hold the vertical axis, of home vs. society. These four cardinal points also function as pivotal portals during a 24-hour day: dawn, midday, dusk, and midnight.

This is an important aspect of the interwoven zodiacal and seasonal cycles, which reveals what an amazing system of Divine Order we live within—the magical dance and interconnection of Heaven and Earth, as John O'Donohue alludes to above. This interpenetration includes not just a mirroring of cycles above and below, but the very makeup of stars, minerals, and animate earthly life, all of which share chemical building blocks. Libra, as an Air sign keen on lofty abstractions, presides over this "beautiful order."

Further, as the seventh sign in the wheel, Libra has the important role of initiating the transition from the self-oriented, personal development of the first six signs to the broader focus of connecting to, and serving, others and the greater whole. For Libra, ruled by the 'love' planet Venus, feedback from others provides a valuable mirror to the self.

It follows, of course, that Libra is known for its charm and sweetness, as it hopes to achieve a pleasing reflection! *Sweetness is the fragrance of the livingness of Life*, go the lyrics of part of Hildegard von Bingen's song, *Spes*, praising the virtue of hope. With world events as they are, to keep hope aloft it's up to each of us in our individual lives to keep the Libran sweetness alive, and keep on sharing it!

Starry emanation of Divine Order at The Alhambra, Granada, Spain

The ripple effect

To fully understand Libra, it's important to consider its relationship with its polarity partner Aries. Theirs is a dance between 'other' and 'self', with too much of either causing a problem. While associated with the balanced scales, Libra does not typically set out as master of its relational realm, but errs either by its people-pleasing and codependence, or its strong-arm Aries willfulness, couched behind moralizing diplomacy. For when off-centered, Libra can devolve to the bellicose lower nature of Aries.

To get centered in its highest potential, Libra's work involves recognizing and shifting entrenched dependency or domination dynamics, either through embracing more of Aries' impulse for freedom and self-assertion, or more of Libra's spirit of harmonious collaboration. Libra also invites us to focus on coming from thoughtful responsiveness, rather than knee-jerk reactivity. In all cases, Libra benefits from accessing its capacity for consideration and tolerance.

The work we do within ourselves in this vein, staunching our disingenuous, impatient, or untamed impulses, to align with our true nature while in relation to others ultimately affects the larger community of life. It starts with ourselves, extends to our friends, family, and networks, and ripples out.

The relational weave—an inside job

For true mastery, relationship work is best undertaken within. A key principle is that of learning to meet one's own needs, and to be one's own support or compass—not looking to or expecting a partner to fulfill these roles. We are not necessarily conditioned in this way, so this takes time, and work. An avenue for this process could involve making a 'sacred marriage' between one's inner masculine and feminine parts, crafting a balance between our outer-directed 'masculine' impulses, and our passive, or receptive, 'feminine' ones.

Typically, in heterosexual relationship chart readings, one looks at a woman's Mars for an indication of the kind of man she's attracted to, and at the man's Venus for the type of woman he's attracted to. (This can hold true for same sex couples when the partners gravitate to one or the other gender expression.) Shamanic astrologer Daniel Giamario suggests that we work on the inner, or sacred, marriage by 'owning' our Mars if female identified, or owning our Venus if male identified. And he suggests we claim the archetypal energies present in our 7th House of relationship. (With no planets there, we would look to the planet ruling the sign on the cusp.)

Often one sees a man's Venus projected onto his partner, and a woman's Mars onto her partner. Owning the relationship signatures in our chart in this way would mean working to embody and live those qualities oneself, not give them to another to act out. This is relevant regardless of whether one is in a committed relationship. Taking myself as an example, my Mars is in Libra. This placement highlights the potential codependent nature of Libra described above—in wanting to assert my instinctual 'masculine' drives (the Mars-Aries impulse) I do so by trying to harmonize and adapt (the Libra-Venus impulse).

Pure Mars energy asserts its desires, and is indifferent to others' needs, but positioned in Libra, its drive could be to prioritize the satisfaction of the partner, friend, or colleague (at least outwardly, or initially!). Therefore, claiming that Mars principle within, instead of relying on a partner to charm and please (or be charmed by), the inner marriage becomes about pleasing oneself! Or as Giamario posits, owning a Mars in Libra means admitting you find your own company the most pleasing of all! (Just something to try on—no astrological principle should be applied without looking at the chart as a whole.)

Out beyond ideas of wrongdoing and right doing
there is a field.
I'll meet you there.
~ Rumi

The mystical relationship

Yet another way of working on the relational balance within is that of making a relationship with God or the Divine. It is this 'field' of Soul, the part of us connected to the All, to which Rumi refers in the poem above—beyond the struggles between right and wrong, beyond all of life's 'tension of the opposites', which provide the heat, or fuel in alchemy. (Wouldn't you know, Rumi was a Libra Sun sign!) In this field we find unity and oneness, and the challenge of fusing our ego persona with our higher self. This realm is described as 'the place where the two seas meet' in the Sufi tale of the mythical Green Man, Khidr, who takes Moses to the place where the two seas meet—where the dead fish becomes alive, and contact with the higher Self becomes a 'living substance' that nourishes the wayfarer—as Sufi teacher Llewellyn Vaughan-Lee describes.[37]

Another perspective on making an inner relationship comes from author and spiritual teacher, A.H. Almaas, founder of *The Ridhwan School,* who frames this in terms of connecting with one's 'essence'. Almaas suggests that deep down, in our personal relationships we harken back to the positive merging we felt with mother as a young infant, but that ultimately, we need to mature into looking within for this satisfaction. He describes our thinking process:

'I have to have somebody who loves me. I have to have somebody who sees me, who values me.' It is true that it is useful and supportive at the beginning, but if you continue depending on it, this will stop you from owning and being who you are. Being who you

are, being your essence, should be completely independent of any other factor, inner or outer…Essence is the life, essence is the fulfillment.[38]

Life in the balance: the fish becomes alive and the two seas meet, Barra, Outer Hebrides

Encountering 'Other,' we are changed

One place where I felt the two seas meet this month was in my first siting of a hummingbird's tongue! I love my garden's denizen 'hummers' (move over hulking military jeeps), and recently noticed a new kid on the branch of my *Arbutus marina* (aka Strawberry) tree, my backyard spot for feathered friend activity. This new hummingbird was more squat, had different coloring—perhaps a male Allen's—and was a riot to watch as he preened and fluffed repeatedly. He then stood stock still as I watched with my binoculars, for many long minutes. Suddenly there emerged from his beak this long, thin, clear beam, shooting far out into the air. What was *that*? I was astounded.

I then discovered a video showing how the hummingbird's tongue splits and feathers at the end, for better sucking power. Witnessing this with no foreknowledge was a blessed phenomenon of finding Heaven *in* Earth, from this miraculous little creature, ever-present in my daily rounds here at home both indoors and out. While I hear her winged whir day and night, on all sides of the house, I had had no knowledge of her tongue!

Further on the 'miraculous earth' theme, we turn to Italian science researcher, author, and 'plant listener,' Monica Gagliano, author of *Thus Spoke the Plant*. Libra loves collaboration, and in a recent podcast, Monica discussed how she works in collaboration with plants and the earth. She points out that "by encountering each other, we change each other." Gagliano strives to open and listen to plants (whom she has determined both speak and make sounds) without preconceived filters, as we do (ideally!) with each other. She also considers planetary change on a vastly bigger scale. "The earth has ideas for rebalancing that we can't conceive of, 300 million years after the First Ice Age."[39]

This affirms my personal musing that, while the delicate balance of Earth's systems has been dangerously affected by human activities, there is still a principle of balance at play. We here in Sonoma County, CA had been struck by destructive wild fires and thick smoke for many weeks of the summer for four years running from 2017-2020, indicating that perhaps our particular climate and ecosystem was 'wired for wildfire', and that it could be time to move.

But right after I explored doing so, the focus shifted. In 2021 we saw the intense fires move up to Oregon and Washington, as well as Canada, and have since had five years' reprieve here, while meanwhile the eastern and central parts of North America, and the world at large, have continued to be hard hit by heat, fires, smoke, and floods. The fierce array of climate disasters seems to be leaving almost no area untouched. One could say that Mother Earth is 'spreading the word', in a balanced way, to all of her corners that we are dreadfully *out of balance*!

Dark side of detachment

The Libra archetype in its highest sense is primed to identify and share beauty and harmony, whether through outer or inner relationship, or artistic expression. Happy playing with (Airy) concepts, it aspires to values and ideals, like justice. However, as said above, Libra does not always *live* or embody its ideals. It might spend time weighing things out, evaluating impulses and actions—its own or others—on the scales of fairness, but then get triggered when it feels its values betrayed, devolving into indignation and even rage, borrowing from hot-headed Aries. At its most off-centered, Libra's self-righteous tantrums turn into the waging of wars in the name of the values to which they are attached.

Autumn colors strike a blessed balance, Laguna de Santa Rosa, Sebastopol, CA

As I write, Israeli President Netanyahu and his cabinet are escalating a new branch of its war, now on Lebanon. One can't help wonder: how can this man persist in this vein of heartless killing? Not knowing his chart, I thought he might have Libra energy (turns out I was right!), as the Libra archetype carries the intense drive after an *ideal* of justice, and this on the level of the conceptual abstract. It thus lacks the feeling capacity, such that the loss of human lives can be taken as a 'necessary consequence' of a 'just' war, with vengeance being justified to right a considered wrong. Air signs are known for their cool detachment.

I then recalled that Vladimir Putin has a Libra Sun sign, and he too is perpetuating a war, driven by the ideal of reinstating the supremacy of 'Mother Russia,' contending that the collapse of the USSR was a "major geopolitical disaster,"[40] with support from the Russian Orthodox Church. At the war's outset, he stated his intent to 'purify' Russia from the harmful Western influences of consumerism and gender/sexual freedoms, among other things.

A review of Putin's chart shows that in addition to the Sun, he has Mercury, Neptune and Saturn all in Libra! Neptune is the other great energy signifying the ideal—on the level of faith, as opposed to Libran reason. Having Neptune conjunct his Sun points to Putin's devotion to his cause and his beliefs. (Off-centered Neptune connected to the Sun can describe someone influenced by deluded dreams.) Several of these Libra planets are trine (in helpful relationship with) Pluto, known in one of its guises as the Destroyer, an energy that doesn't shy from applying violence and killing to achieve its goal of deep transformation.

Then I found Netanyahu's chart, where I struck astrological pay dirt (for purposes of my exploration, that is)! He *too* has Sun, Mercury, and Neptune in Libra, along with his Moon and South Node (where he's coming from in the past). Several of his Libra planets are trine Pluto as well, which shows how, like Putin, he does not balk at using ruthless violence to achieve his calculated 'rational' ends. While Netanyahu's ideal/ideology differs from Putin's, both stem from a sense of injustice (however distorted by Neptune), of their people having been wronged or robbed of their rightful place and role on the planet.

The Sun-Neptune conjunction in Libra they both have calls in an identification with the 'glorious ones', those who have suffered through being downtrodden or deprived of their exalted birthright, identifying with loss and victimhood, and 'justifying' gross levels of perpetration.

Wondering at the 'things' of life

In the name of keeping a balanced mind-body-spirit, it's important in these times to dwell on politics only in small bites, as the topic can raise the blood pressure precipitously! Calling us back homewards and earthwards, I want to consider a lovely fall equinox ritual I attended last week in our local Ragle Ranch Park. The facilitators invited us to spend some time listening to a chosen part of our surroundings (I chose an impressively sprawling, moss-adorned oak), inquiring what energy is beckoning to us this fall. Some of the qualities called out when we returned to the circle to share were: acceptance, gratitude, and letting go.

Fall is a time of consolidation, of gathering and drawing ourselves into the sphere of focused relationship and interior life. It is a time of sorting and sifting through the remains of the harvest, of the trees releasing their spent leaves, and our own letting go of that which has withered and is no longer needed—perhaps outworn habits, or ways of thinking about ourselves.

Virgo, the preceding sign, is in its own way called to the work of purifying and integrating various aspects of the self. Now, with Libra, we take that integrated self and reach out, whether through social connection, or through the arts, to extend our sense of beauty, and our refined values, to others. While yes, in its darkest manifestation, Libra can be a cold and calculating war-monger, in its highest, given its association with the goddess Aphrodite (the Greek name for Venus), beauty, love, and harmony emerge. Experiences of aesthetic intensity, such as with the Earth, bring us a sense of our essential values, helping us to a deeper knowing of the import of the 'things' of this life. From here, we are led to gratitude.

Persimmons, earthly 'things', branded by stars

Pondering 'the things of life,' I think of the acclaimed book, *The Matter with Things*[41], by Iain McGilchrist, brilliant British psychiatrist, philosopher and neuroscientist (and author of the previous *The Master and His Emissary,* about the distinctions between the left and right hemispheres of the brain). In both works, McGilchrist points to the increasingly imbalanced focus in the Western world on the conceptual thinking mind and its constructs. The detached mind's purview is the left brain, which we could say over favors the Air signs' detached, rational approach to life. So while Libra in its origins aspires for divine order and harmony, it needs rectifying in these times, as its dissociation from material reality and other ways of knowing has gone too far aloft!

In an online interview, McGilchrist stresses that our 'enslavement' to the left hemisphere's view of things, at the expense of the intuitive, creative, whole-perceiving right brain is responsible for the downfall of many aspects of modern life. He exhorts us to more concertedly embrace the right hemisphere's gifts of intuition, imagination, and awe, which afford us a lens on life that "is both profound and beautiful—and happens to be in line with the deepest traditions of human wisdom." Here is where the Libran propensity for measuring needs to yield to its innate connection to the Causal, or Imaginal, realm—where archetypes originate—through dwelling in its passion for the beautiful.

Held in the balance

Libra does best when it keeps to its higher ideals, which means ever looking to the "pattern of Order and Beauty," which John O'Donohue speaks of, in our navigations through life, and not getting bogged down in the muck of opinionated pundits and doomed forecasts. Here's where a healthy dose of Libran detachment can be of good use!

Keeping our aim trained on our highest ideals requires that we invoke our reasoning powers when considering options. For instance, when stating boundaries and limits, sometimes it's best to err on the side of tolerance when we feel wronged; at others, we may need to draw the line out of self-respect, stating why a certain dynamic simply isn't acceptable, to prevent the build-up of resentment. This might require some Aries 'hutzpah', as Libra is far more comfortable with accommodating others!

Because of its preference for pleasing, Libra can be prone to rethinking and even reneging on its stated boundaries. (I surely did this in my parenting journey, with both my Mars and Mercury in Libra). Children as a general rule do *need* strong boundaries to feel safe, so having 'soft boundaries' ongoingly can invite more acting out. Getting the balance right between control and surrender, structure and flow, is ever a work in progress, and requires nuanced adjusting.

Another challenge that Libra deals with is the weighing of pros and cons in making decisions—not per se its forte! In the highest sense, Libra calls us to make choices that will respect the natural laws and rhythms of the earth, and to honor our notion of divine order, whether materially or morally. But in our mundane lives, we are at times called to the difficult task of *choosing* in situations such as whether to stay at a stressful job, whether to embark on a course of higher education, or where to go on vacation!

Moon in the balance, with dahlias, at Sonoma County Harvest Fair

Choosing necessitates rejecting one option, and excluding psychic content that may be wrapped around it—content that can lurk beneath, only to rise later and cause disruption if it turns out the choice made wasn't aligned with our soul's intent. The classic 'waffling' that Libra falls into stems in part from the fear of the consequences—particularly commitment. What will be lost or left behind? What will we face in this situation/person that we have chosen? Jungian astrologer Liz Greene points out that Libra energy is called to the fore in situations where we may be forced to make choices that divide ourselves. These press us to determine where our true values lie, deepening our self-knowledge, and encouraging us to overcome instincts that may not be ethically founded, or the most 'beautiful'.[42]

To give or not to give

In addition to Aphrodite, Libra is associated with the Greek goddess Athena in her preoccupation with law, social order, and care for the community. In the Athena aspect we see

Libra's interest in law and society, as opposed to self and family. We also see the concern with broken rules and injustice!

The Greek gods were prone to all sorts of tantrums and retaliations over things relational, similar to the Old Testament Yahweh, as depicted by Carl Jung in his book, *Answer To Job*.[43] Having recently finished reading this, I was struck that when I explored Liz Greene's archetypal analysis of Libra, her take on Libra themes echoed those outlined in Jung's book. (Greene even overtly makes the connection between Libra and this book.)

In short, Jung describes that Yahweh, or God/the Creator is not at all perfect. In fact, he, like the Greek gods, is partly unconscious, making him 'two-faced', and perhaps not as just as a 'good human'. Job, a shining human example, had in fact surpassed God in this respect, Jung posits. Hence the gods, or the Creator, have turned to and need humankind to be the place for seeding a truly moral consciousness. In this respect, while Libra can, as we've established, encompass the lowest of human behaviors when it gives itself over to the purely abstract, calculating ideal of retribution, it can also lead the way to the noblest of roles, that of improving upon God!

But lest we get too carried away over the elevated potential of Libra, Greene points out that "the development of Libra encompasses a curious paradox: that the sign is in love with the orderly laws of life and places great faith in their fairness, yet is perpetually confronted by the disorderly and immoral aspects of life, which fragment and divide Libra's cherished unity."[44]

Sometimes Libra gets bogged down with over-giving, for instance, and then later resents how the recipient doesn't reciprocate in kind. This is a tough one, as not everyone is graced with the Libran energy that prioritizes the consideration of others, and as equals. Fire sign energy, in particular (Aries, Leo, Sagittarius), can be quite self-focused, burning its own bright light, with not much energy spent on empathy. Eventually, with enough unrequited giving, kindness, and prioritizing of the needs of magnetic others, Libra gets fed up and blows a fuse.

As alluded to above, to prevent this, the guidance for Libra is to borrow from its Aries polarity partner's self-focus, to take care of oneself by presencing its needs, and refrain from hoping or expecting that others will take care of them. Libra goes astray when it thinks its needs are another's responsibility (or that another's needs are its responsibility!)

Revered humanistic astrologer Dane Rudhyar points out that while ever striving towards equilibrium, and towards finding a desired social sphere or group where it feels it fits in and belongs, Libra is often subject to instability, feeling itself continually falling short of the mark. For it is neither a master of balance, *nor* of the social process; hence it must continually strive in both realms. Ultimately, Rudhyar asserts, Libra is more an artist than a politician, more a seer and a harmonizer than a builder.[45] I find it helpful to consider this, that it is not Libra's work to 'achieve', per se, but to imbue. Rudhyar compares Libra to a seed, a love-inspired seed, infused with wisdom, whose work is to disseminate into humanity its vision of peace, order, and beauty.

Considering the breath as another aspect of Libra's Airy domain, we might then consider that with each conscious breath taken—conscious and aware of the divine harmony that is our human potential—Libra can infuse our planet, and its inhabitants with whom we share it, with love. Libra thus offers the possibility of the seed of consciousness, of goodness, of morality, which in its highest manifestation would be an Earth in balance.

Acorns: seeds packed tight with the Idea of Oak

"The bubbling lightness of plenty"

Of course, we have likely many centuries to go with the work of restoring our Earth to her original state of homeostasis from which it has precipitously strayed. While many eyes are trained on technology as the god that can save us from global warming's rapidly escalating environmental stressors and catastrophes, 'green energy' is in some respects a suspect savior.

In a persuasive article on the negative effects of offshore wind energy,[46] Erica Shugart points to wind energy's lesser-known consequences, which include harm to sea life and marine ecosystems, and habitat and mineral loss from the use of resources to build the turbines. She describes the mere 15 to 20-year lifespan of wind turbines, which cannot be recycled or broken down once they fail, and which can cause very significant damages to ecosystems when they do fail. In Libran fashion, she raises the question, is it a 'lesser evil' to kill whales with industrial wind energy than by fossil fuel-induced global warming? She writes:

> *A protean trickster, industry changes shape and name, but the blight it forges belongs to a legacy that arose long before industrial fossil fuel extraction. This [green energy] solution promises salvation, cloaked by a technical language that leaves one hoping that the experts will soon be arriving. Hidden beneath the false double bind are count-less ways that communities could re-localize and become more aligned with Earth.*

My sense is that at some point we'll be forced to return to a far less resource-intensive, simpler way of localized living, in balance with Earth's resources and cycles, and that tech-nology—and the continued mining of the earth for its components—is not a viable panacea. Living in respect for the earth and her limitations, and for all beings with whom we share it, is what Indigenous peoples have always done, and what our ancestors to varying degrees have done as well. Simple living is the only way to strike a balance within our now perilously threatened web of earth systems. Shugart beautifully states:

> *Some of us may have forgotten that intrinsic to sustainable cultures, obligation lies not with distant figures, mandates, or machines, but with place wisdom passed down by the ancestors who have returned to spaciousness. Part of the work as brief Earthlings might be to understand that honoring physical limitation is the door to the bubbling lightness of plenty known as gratitude.*

SEEING IN THE DARK: SCORPIO

~ October 23-November 21

The call towards darkness is upon us—both seasonally as we approach winter, and archetypally with the Sun abiding in Scorpio, the explorer of the difficult depths. Many of us may resist—even resent—this turn towards darkening days, a turn made more acute by the 'portal' our culture has devised that is the end of Daylight Savings Time, summoning an extra dollop of darkness. Ouch!

As natural lovers of the Sun, many of us instinctively favor the days and early evenings spent in the warm, illuminated outdoors, where we can absorb the life-giving Sun's fire, and interact with the other intelligent beings and elements of the earth's day world. But now, with cooling nights and shortened days at hand, we are called back to the other side of the rhythmic cycle of life, the death side—the side that migrates towards, and merges with, darkness and shadow.

Scorpio's polarity partner, Taurus, the grounded Earth sign part of us, finds its joy and its meaning, and as well its very spirituality, in matter/*mater* (Latin for mother). This includes Mother Earth's soils, rocks, plant life, animal kin, and the immersion in our own physical senses. So to the above-ground, Earth lover in us, it's almost wrenching when Water sign Scorpio calls us within, to an arena less familiar, and potentially more threatening, signified by that which lies below ground. To a place we call the Underworld.

This realm includes those deep feelings and provocative memories from early childhood that we have repressed from our conscious minds, and which occasionally resurface in surprise moments as adults. The pushing down of that which was too painful to bear when we experienced our first wound of separation (the 'wounded healer, asteroid Chiron being a primary significator thereof) was a very necessary survival strategy when we were young, but eventually, if we are on a path to wholeness, as adults we are tasked with facing and releasing what is buried in the unconscious. Otherwise, these memories and emotions keep part of our creative, energetic life force locked up and inaccessible.

The courage to look within

Last night, in perfect synchrony with these observations, I was invited to watch a candid podcast conversation between CNN anchor Anderson Cooper and grief psychotherapist Francis Weller.[47] Presented as a podcast interview, it was more like a recap of the therapy work the two have been doing together through time, in which Weller points to and elaborates on some of the concepts I'd described above. (Psychological practices are signified by the sign Scorpio, given that they involve inner excavation for hidden gems of truth—often hard won, which in turn bring healing.)

In the podcast, Cooper boldly bares his inner pain over the 40-years-on loss of his father, and the revelation that the ensuing strategies that had helped him successfully 'hold down a job' (a spotlit one at that!) were no longer useful. Is not much of our world like that? With polished, statuesque appearances belying a teeming sea of hidden emotions, struggles, memories, and aspirations? He professes his own 'Come to Jesus' moment about this.

I applaud Anderson for sharing this exchange with the world, and for exposing his own feelings and vulnerability over his losses. I highly recommend listening to the conversation, especially if you are inclined to the difficult and tender work of being with, and "turning over the compost" of your grief, as Weller says.

Compost is itself a potent significator of Scorpio, as it involves the process of regenerating our cast-off waste—physically speaking, as rich nourishment for soils, and emotionally speaking, as the tears, anger, and fear that we reject for not being part of 'the good stuff' we think we're striving for, but which in fact are nutrients for transformative processes. Compost is a vital source of nourishment for renewed, and healed, life.

Paradise lost

Fundamentally, our wound of separation centers in some way around grief over our *Paradise Lost* (interestingly the author of that tome, John Milton, had Scorpio rising, as did the founder of psychoanalysis, Sigmund Freud. The rising sign significantly informs the persona, and thereby the nature of our journey through life.) And while Pisces too presides over loss, Scorpio's is the archetypal season that invites us to dig into our losses, our traumas, our falls from grace, and engage with the work of dissolving our encrusted and calcified coping strategies—coined as 'complexes' by C.G. Jung, and otherwise known as default ego patterns.

Looking at our unconscious patterning is difficult work, and calls in the Scorpio qualities of courageous inquiry and perseverance. Engaging with this process can feel threatening, but it is paramount if we are to grow the robust resilience that is and will continue to be needed as we face the radical changes afoot on our planet. Without such healing work, we will be at the whims of our more primitive reactions to perceived threats. But when we have fully embraced our inner demons, allowed ourselves to become 'undone,' and found our way back, we are ready to hold steady when outer perils arise.

The major news headlines are already replete with such perils, at the now-mythic level, whether of genocidal war, autocratic forces, economic fragility, and environmental catastrophes. However, these are but part of the story of our time—the dark one. There is another movement afoot, that of awakening into the light, equally apace, albeit hidden. Ironically, this one requires an embrace of the dark, if it is to be experienced.

If you've been reading through these chapters consecutively, you are by now familiar with the myth of Hades' abduction of the innocent maiden Persephone, Demeter's daughter, down to his kingdom below, while she was out picking flowers in the field. This abduction was not in the plan...or was it? [I've referenced this in the Cancer and Virgo chapters, and now here as well, as the theme of abduction into the underworld relates to Scorpio. All three of these are archetypes pertaining to the deep Feminine.]

Jungian astrologer Liz Greene[48] suggests that an unconscious part of Persephone longed for this experience, in the name of attaining wholeness; that part of her wanted or at least needed the experience of the Underworld. Hence her choosing to eat the forbidden seeds of pomegranate while leaving Hades, which fated her to return for part of the year ever after. For the darkness—our pain and suffering, the trauma we have repressed in order to function in the world—is part of life. It hits us all in one way or another, this call to suffering, this seemingly haphazard fall into the realm of whatever pain we may be asked to confront. If it does not, and we continue to suppress our wounds, we live only part of our true potential.

It is by facing the shadows within (where it's darkest of all!), such as Jung did over the five years he chronicled in *The Red Book: Liber Novus*[49], that we can ultimately achieve a type of renewal from the core of our being. No less than this is what the Scorpio archetype, with Pluto as its modern ruler, ultimately asks of us.

Shedding the skin

In step with the inward pull, I have been studying *The Red Book* lately from the perspective of its underlying astrological associations, including some of the color plates of the evocative images Jung painted depicting his meetings with Underworld characters that came to figure as members of his inner pantheon.[50] Entering into sustained inner dialogue with them, he gained great wisdom, and ultimately achieved the type of transformation that Scorpio calls us to. While some had termed this phase of Jung's life a 'psychotic break,' from his standpoint and that of psychological practitioners who embrace shadow work, this was a deeply courageous act, one of turning wholeheartedly within, with body, mind, and soul, at a time when he was feeling deeply fragmented and uncertain.

One of my early paintings, featuring images of birth and death

As someone with a fair share of Scorpio-Pluto energy myself (although no actual planets in Scorpio), I have always felt at home at this time of year, and with the exploration of psychological depths. Perhaps also testament to my Scorpio (as well as Pisces) bent, I have done my own exploration of my inner world via the creative imagination, through earlier years spent with *The Painting Experience* practice, founded by Michelle Cassou. This powerful and influential creative process wove itself into my first encounter with Sufism, and together the two ushered me through my first Saturn return, leading to a complete change of life.

Once could say this was a type of death and rebirth time, the shedding of an old skin, with the snake being a significator of Scorpio. While only some rare humans behave like slithering serpents (I have encountered one, a crooked tax accountant!), we humans do engage in shedding of skins, to greater and lesser degrees, depending on the cycles at hand. For me, this time of 'greater' transformation was marked by Pluto in Scorpio crossing over my Scorpio ascendant. For the rest of us, during Scorpio season, even if we don't have a major Pluto transit on hand, we are certainly dancing with the archetypal forces of transformation.

Fiery Mars, geared to take action on behalf of our passions and desires, is Scorpio's traditional ruler, and Pluto its modern ruler. Pluto entered Aquarius for a 20-year stay in November 2024, marking a significant epochal change. One of Scorpio/Pluto's signatures is the struggle between power and powerlessness.

With Pluto now traversing the early degrees of the sign of 'change' (change agent Uranus being Aquarius' modern ruler) we find ourselves in an intense and *power*ful time as old methods and systems of power either intensify or fall away. We ourselves are called to access our deepest instinctual self, signified by the Mars/Aries archetype, particularly with 'wounded healer' Chiron positioned in Aries until April 2027 (with 3 months in Taurus in 2026). Pluto in Aquarius calls us to new horizons and new frameworks, and Chiron in Aries asks us to step up to the plate, courageously claiming our role in the planetary changes afoot.

But before we can accomplish this, we need heed Scorpio's call to the undefended depths, which challenges us to take risks, whether to our reputation, or our very sense of self, through facing the truths we (or others) may have buried. WikiLeaks founder Julian Assange is one such courageous warrior, a journalist known for his fearless uncovering of information concealing probable war crimes by the US Army. Interesting that both he and Cooper are Scorpio journalists, unafraid of putting themselves in harm's way to reveal the truth, each in their own way.

Seeds of truth

Cooper has 'excavator' Pluto squaring his 8th House Sun (the 8th House being naturally ruled by Scorpio), and his Moon's South Node in Scorpio. With the 8th house being the area of life where all manner of shadowy, emotion-laden matters arise, and the South Node describing our past 'proficiencies,' his chart suggests he incarnated with a great deal of familiarity with the difficult realms of Scorpio, and had 'signed up' for more. Julian Assange, likewise, has his Sun in the 8th house, and his Moon (instinctual, emotional self) and Jupiter (our philosophical frame) in Scorpio. Another aspect of Scorpio is that it is in relentless pursuit of hidden truths.

Fated pomegranate seeds: implicated in the Persephone abduction myth

Sadly, Assange has indeed faced the darkness in this pursuit, suffering greatly from the torture and isolation he endured over five years in British prison for his 'crime' of exposing hidden information. Esteemed mythologist Michael Meade, who himself served time for his opposition to the Vietnam war describes prison time as an Underworld initiation, which for him was one of both indescribable darkness and his greatest awakening. Assange was released in summer 2024 on a plea deal, in which he had to confess to this 'crime,' in order to be set free. "I am not free today because the system worked. I am free today," he said in a public news conference, "after years of incarceration, because I pled guilty to journalism."

Scorpio energy need not always be this brutal, but it is definitely not for the faint of heart. Its processes, while ostensibly destructive, are intended for rebirth, to which its highest totem, the phoenix (riser from the ashes), testifies. As Meade stated in an online webinar,

"The Soul of Change,"[51] "The emotions enter us to change us…the growth of the soul finds its balance through experiencing extremes."

Meade points to the earth, and nature itself, as a great force of change and transformation, with the pinnacle of its metamorphosing impulses being that of caterpillar to butterfly. The ancient Greeks used the word psyche to connote the butterfly, and given that in depth psychology we equate soul with the human psyche, we see that the butterfly's biological rebirth is in fact a mythological story of transformation. The amazing fact about this, Meade points out, is that the cells in the caterpillar *resist* and even try to kill the butterfly-programmed cells, which are called the "imago." Even more amazing (and heart-warming!) is that the attack mounted by the caterpillar cells, which are trying to protect its many-legged status quo, actually *strengthens* the growth capacity of the butterfly.

Resistance training

In this light, we see how resistance to change is part and parcel of change. All of this plays out in our human lives as well. Our resistance (or revulsion) towards change comes disguised as deep fears and ego attitudes. "Becoming who we truly are, following the natural drive of the Soul, is the hardest thing we'll ever do," Meade attests. We have to loosen the grip of the ego, allow the deeper Self to fill the places within.

> *Initiation is a revelation from within, a revealing of oneself to oneself. Each crisis brings us closer to awakening. The 'inner initiate' in us [the Scorpio energy], knows that to be healed—to become more whole, more creative, so that we can add meaning to the world—something in us has to die, in order for something else to be born.*

But death by necessity precedes rebirth, and ours is a dying time. Many I know are facing the loss of loved ones, of relationships, of beloved places, of homes inhabited and cherished for years, of good health, of youth! And the earth, too, in this moment, feels more than ever to be dying, after an early autumn of extended, crushing heat here has roasted leaves and vines to a crisp. World-wide, many regions have been feeling even worse tolls from intense heat.

Embracing the wasteland

The other day I was walking at my local Laguna de Santa Rosa, heretofore always a place of uplifting vistas, colors, and vibrant plant and birdlife. This time I found a type of wasteland.

I'd been walking but 10 minutes when I was brutally stung twice, by an invisible and inaudible Scorpionic stinger, behind my knee and on my rear. I cried out, the pain was so acute. (The expansive, red, stinging rash lasted days.) I haven't experienced a sting, such as by a bee, in a couple of decades. And I was wearing long, thick pants, so I have no idea how the perpetrator gained access.

I continued walking anyway, only to discover the seasonal bridge I'd planned to cross over the Laguna waterway had been taken down. As I turned and headed back to my car, I noticed the hardened, gray-brown earth, which in spring hosts golden California poppies and soft grasses, was deadened but for a thick, traveling weed. Amidst the weedy vines I startled at the sight of a bright green, 9-inch lizard with a gaping jaw, near my feet. My own private Underworld! I then realized it was a rubber lizard, deposited by some Trickster.

Somehow this all feels very consonant with the time—so much not being as it once was, as we've come to expect. We are really and truly being called to a new level of strength, and to deepen in our work of pursuing Beauty in all places. As Rainer Maria Rilke insists in one of his *Letters To a Young Poet*, "everywhere there is much beauty."[52] If so, we are tasked more than ever with finding it, even in the dying places. I got back in my car and drove to the other side of the Laguna to continue my walk, where I found a simple beauty, in the rhythm of my legs traversing the dusty path, surrounded by the spaciousness of land and sky, and a few muted but evident colors.

Scorpio presides over extremes of mythic heights and depths (some of us may know this one in our relationships!). Here in my little Underworld nature outing, I had met with some drama as well. But this is surely meaningful, taken through the lens of finding meaning in all things, as a sort of light in the darkness, a taking of the hand of the Creator/Beloved. *The Gene Keys* author and visionary, Richard Rudd, sums it up in some words he shared online about our time:

> *The mythic is even played out on a mundane level, but only when we give ourselves totally to the drama. This is the beautiful metaphor of drama, and it's why we are so drawn to it, because it contains the codes of transformation. All drama has transformation woven into it, and that transformation always moves into higher and higher frequencies as the dark nature reveals its hidden light.*[53]

A footnote to the above 'wasteland' drama: just upon completing this chapter, a year after I'd originally written the above section for my blog, the local paper offered an article about a "Teen Labyrinth of Life" that has been created by a church group and city government officials, in honor of local teens who had lost or taken their lives. The labyrinth is in the very area where I was stung, and saw the giant lizard, at the edge of the Laguna. A notably positive and unexpected denouement of this waking dream—may this be an indicator of times ahead!

Keep Calm and Carry On

If we approach the dramas of our lives with perspective, and inner awareness, we can help facilitate the transformational 'weave' Rudd speaks of, and choose to live with more light in our hearts and minds. But this takes time, and in Scorpio season, we have months of darkened days ahead. We must remember to breathe deeply and harness patience for the journey.

In this season falls the important cross-quarter day of *Samhain* (Sow-win), equidistant between the fall equinox and winter solstice. For the Celts of Ireland and the British Isles (and of French Gaul and Spanish Galicia in ancient times), Samhain marked the end of the harvest, and the start of the New Year—the opening to Winter, and the time

of darkness. It is the time of year when the 'veils are thinnest' between this world and the next, hence *Day of the Dead* and *All Soul's Day* falling right afterwards. Bonfires were traditionally lit to help keep out the dark spirits that roamed.

This year I am noticing that almost all the front yard Hallowe'en displays feature a pronounced focus on the death theme, with multiplying R.I.P. gravestones and skeletons of all shapes and sizes, one a scene of bloody slaughter and a placard reading, *Keep Calm and Carrion*. I was moved to join in and put up a skeleton my grown daughter had fashioned from cardboard and shells, in kindergarten, in honor of what cannot be denied in this time.

Getting grounded in the body, and with the outdoor elements (the slant of light these days like golden honey) are always good ideas when things feel grim. Today in my Qi Gong class we did a repetitive circular movement that embodies the birth and death wheel of life, and we closed with a meditation that brought the reality of "down and in," which is the energy of the time both earth-wise and archetypally, into our bodies in a grounding way. I find that staying present with the body, and practicing gentleness with ourselves through whatever ups and downs come our way is a beautiful medicine to help us through.

The Turn Within

Unison Benediction

Return to the most human,
nothing less will nourish the torn spirit,
the bewildered heart, the angry mind;
and from the ultimate duress,
pierced with the breath of anguish,
speak of love.

Return, return to the deep sources,
nothing less will teach the stiff hands a new way to serve,
to carve into our lives the forms of tenderness
and still that ancient necessary pain preserve.

Return to the most human,
nothing less will teach the angry spirit,
the bewildered heart, the torn mind,
to accept the whole of its duress,
and pierced with anguish...
at last, act for love.[54]
~ May Sarton

As we've established, Water sign Scorpio's season is indeed a time, as May Sarton indicates, to "return to the deep sources" and face our grievances and our grief. And it wants us to do so *with feeling*. If this is hard for us to do, we mustn't be surprised if life throws us a fireball or two to get us in the mood. When we feel violated or betrayed, or triggered into untamable rage, we are in Scorpionic waters. Yet aggravation and violation are but part of the Scorpio archetype—its opening act or, if left unfinished, its lower octave. The rest is about regeneration, healing, and rebirth. This brings me to some wise words from Christian mystic, Father Thomas Keating, known for his development of the practice of Contemplative Prayer.

> *Powerlessness is our greatest treasure. Don't try to get rid of it. Everything in us wants to get rid of it. Grace is sufficient for you, but not something you can understand. To be in too big a hurry to get over our difficulties is a mistake because you don't know how valuable they are from God's perspective, for without them you might never be transformed as deeply and as thoroughly.*

This reflection offers a very different take on Scorpio medicine, pointing us to its 'high road.' Transformation is the deepest intent of Scorpio and Pluto, and as said, this often requires that we visit, and spend time with the much-feared realms of powerlessness. For Scorpio's purifying methods often bring death to ego power, and to power *over*, in order to birth within us the abiding power of love. Love is the power that helps us accept what is and what is not, helping us take our place in the presence of God, Essence, Creator—however we might describe it.

When Father Keating says "grace is sufficient, but not something you can understand," he is really pointing to the path of surrender, to the need to open to trusting the grace in the 'slings and arrows' of life, with an understanding that these are our healers in disguise, pointing us to vital truths about ourselves.

Scorpio walking

I've made several 'Scorpio Walking' sightings in media offerings this season. First is a series called *Shrinking*, on Apple TV, that I learned about from UC Berkeley's online *Greater Good Magazine* in an article spotlighting shows that 'help us be our best self.' As you might guess, *Shrinking* is about a therapist—several actually, one of whom is played by Harrison Ford.

I have to laugh, that this acclaimed tough guy actor, known for his roles in action thrillers like *Raiders of the Lost Ark* and *The Fugitive* is now, at his well-seasoned age, playing the role of chief therapist, focusing at last on the 'drama within,' realizing that he himself has grief and loss he hasn't processed. As do the other two therapists in his office.

One of them has lost his wife the prior year and has resisted facing his pain, which of course echoes in the stuckness he feels in his client work. He finally decides to 'go for the jugular' with his clients, to boldly share the truth about what he sees going on, using unorthodox means, and to finally do his own work on himself. It's a perfect Scorpio message, that we *all* have work to do examining our 'shadows,' on that which has been repressed, and we have to be fearless about it. This is key to liberation from frozenness and pain.

Along these lines, there was a statement by *OnBeing* podcast host, Krista Tippett, that caught my attention recently. She said, "the definition of a deep truth is that its opposite is also true." This would mean that Light is a truth only if Darkness is also embraced as a truth. They need each other to be understood. Scorpio energy beckons us to claim the riches of this notion.

Also on the air waves, I noticed a new Metropolitan opera production of the 1995 film *Dead Man Walking,* about the powerfully redemptive accompaniment offered by Sister Helen Prejan of a condemned murderer on Death Row. The story illustrates the Scorpionic theme of finding courage to face taboos in the name of healing, and redemption in the face of death.

Fallen Tithonia (Mexican sunflower) in her dying days

The Endless Cycle

Coming back to earth with my investigative Scorpio spy glass, I learned on a recent guided birding outing that the Latin name for the oft-maligned Turkey vulture, *Cathartes aura,* means 'purifying breeze.' Given that these birds do us the service of devouring and digesting dead animal remains, this red-headed raptor seems a perfect Scorpio agent—embracing the dead, using the remains as fodder, and purifying (the landscape) in the process.

Here at home, I have been audience to the persistent work of the Orb spider, always active in the fall. This year for the first time one of these chose to cast her web on the frame of my kitchen sink window—I guess she wanted my attention! For several weeks from my dishwashing station I got to watch her comings and goings, and adventures with her prey, until one day we had a significant rain, which knocked out 2/3 of her web. I thought for sure it was curtains for Mme Orb's window web. But, never say die to a spider! Undaunted by the elements, the next morning the web was back up in full (if not perfect) symmetry.

Stepping back to take the long view of transformation and change that Pluto in Aquarius indicates can be a helpful balm during moments of emotional trials. For a truly big picture perspective on this death/rebirth cycle, eco-philosopher David Hinton provocatively posits that what's happening now with climate collapse, aka the Sixth Great Extinction, is a "completely natural event."[55]

> *It's the way of things, appearing and flourishing and vanishing: animals, food webs, mountain ranges, continents, stars and galaxies, and also the diversity of earth's planetary ecosystems. Transformation always involves destruction, that vanishing of things that allows new configurations of existence to arise. It's even there in the moment-to-moment vanishing of thoughts and perceptions within consciousness, always opening space for new thoughts and perceptions.*

Looking at the crisis of the earth's systems in this way is a decidedly detached approach, not so Scorpionic, but more the style of an Air sign. Combining both Water and Air sign impulses, ideally we allow in the grief over the earth's losses, and those within ourselves, with the Watery moisture of our tears, in order to then, cleansed and purified, enter that detached Aquarian "space for new thoughts and perceptions" that Hinton beckons us to. Perhaps we will find there are changes we want to make in how we orient our lives, and how we frame perceptions going forward, regardless of circumstances.

Refining our Beliefs: Sagittarius

~ November 22-December 21

Winter cold and stillness are upon us, the leaves steadily flying from the trees. Prepping for my Sagittarius class, I am reminded that the mighty oak is one of Jupiter's totems (Jupiter being the ruler of Sagittarius). Fitting as, at this time here in my watershed we are gifted with a diverse array of oak leaf shapes and colors, fluttering in the winds, sparkling on trees after rains, and carpeting the ground in soft gold. (I so love shuffling through them!)

After a particularly brutal Scorpio season on the world stage, it surely amazes to now find ourselves infused with the sharply contrasting Sagittarius themes of hope, vision, and faith that the 'Archer' brings. The Wheel of Life does not rest for long in one groove, we find.

Call to joy—A shift in the memes

Despite whatever darkness still lurks in the news cycle, when the Sun enters Sagittarius, there can be a notable shift in the memes. These now include a call to joy and hope, two prominent themes of the archetype. All the more appropriate, with the holidays at hand, when we are called to raise our voices in song, or tune in to 'choirs of angels.' Although we may be called to a rewrite on the importance of 'the holidays' in these times. Regardless, I'm feeling acutely how the corrective medicine of upbeat Sagittarius (which each sign offers as an antidote to the extremes of its predecessor) is truly a necessary and healing balm.

I recently tuned in to an inspiring podcast conversation involving Irish writer, Kerry Ni Dochartaigh (author of *Thin Times*), which homes in on these messages. "To allow joy to come and sit close is a very political act—to sit in the light that can only exist because of the darkness," Kerry says. She points to the need to find hope in the big picture view of life, a project that Sagittarius is keen to tackle. "Allowing hope and joy is a quick-fire way to open to heart-centeredness and growth," she adds.

Growth, kin to expansiveness, is another core feature of Sagittarius/Jupiter energy. Upwards and outwards, the courageous adventurer's cry rallies, undeterred by setbacks and failings, continuing on in the quest for enlightening visions and ideas.

Ni Dochartaigh also touches on the pursuit of truth, a calling of both Sagittarius and Scorpio, each in their own way. Scorpio asks us to surrender to the truth of that which causes pain, as part of healing and regeneration. At its best, it stands ready to face down, feel, and excavate repressed traumas, unafraid of opening to the suffering that such truth may impart. Sagittarius, in contrast, is after a transcendent, over-arching truth, one that can guide our lives by grounding it in our hearts and in our seeing, perhaps first encountering it in high places—whether these be a mountaintop, a meditation cushion, or a seat of advanced learning.

A recent newsletter from author, theologian, and activist priest, Matthew Fox[56] echoes the call to noble aspirations. Speaking to the horrific wars of the time, Fox asserts that joy is deeper than sorrow and grief, and that it is found not by banishing suffering, but by going still deeper.

"The *via postiva* sustains us when the *via negativa* tends to swamp us and take over." No doubt Fox's Sagittarius placements—Sun, Venus, Mercury—with the Sun squaring Neptune, helps fortify his faith in goodness and nobility, and fund the capacity to rise above darkness. Key to the endeavor of rising from darkness, however, is that it not be a spiritual bypass—one of the potential pitfalls of the high-minded Sagittarius pulse.

The compass of meaning—Viktor Frankl

While many untold oppressed individuals have managed to find a sustaining light within bleak darkness, only a few have achieved fame in so doing. Viktor Frankl, holocaust survivor and author of the impactful book, *Man's Search for Meaning,* may be the most renowned. In an online interview he shares his secret for surviving the horrors he lived through.

He who has a why to live for can bear almost any how. The will-to-meaning, the will to find and to fulfill meaning, is the basic motivation in a human being.

Meaning-making is one of Sagittarius's major concerns. Frankl himself had an optimistic Sagittarius Moon opposite Pluto, planet of 'death and transformation' (and ruler of Scorpio), which certainly speaks to his capacity to rise from the ashes of his experience through focusing on the light of meaning. He found this light in both witnessing and engaging in creative pursuits while in the camps, as well as in serving and caring for others in their despair in his capacity as a psychiatrist. All of this helped him achieve a level of balance amidst the grueling losses he endured and was surrounded by.

While meaning can take many forms, Sagittarius often aims for the prize through the synthesis of knowledge and ideas into a larger system of understanding (such as religion, law, spiritual philosophy, or astrology). However, Sagittarius is a Fire sign. As such, its mode of accessing truth is the intuition, not the mind. Hence its connection with the Teacher or wisdom guide, such as the Wise Men in the story of Jesus's birth, guided not by book knowledge, but by the light of a star.

From the heart to the universe—Thomas Berry

In this vein, I came upon a recent interview with another great way-shower of our time, Thomas Berry—cultural historian, world religions scholar, geologist, and staunch advocate for protecting the earth's integral systems. In the article[57] Berry speaks with great eloquence to the value of intuitive consciousness.

> *We have the capacity to awaken to the inner life of things. It is about another way of knowing, an 'origin-al' way of knowing, you might say. It is a knowing that is connected as a tendril of the heart to the heart of the universe. It is a numinous awareness, an intuitive consciousness, a second voice, which resides beneath the rational faculties and is actually the approach to transformation.*

Throughout his long life, Berry determinedly spread his vision of human interdependence with the earth as part of the unfolding journey of the universe. Something that Indigenous peoples have known and lived for tens of thousands of years, which is why we are increasingly turning to them as the last, vital repositories of how to establish a truly 'ecological civilization.'

'Muscular Hope'—Christiana Figueres

A powerful advocate for shifting wayward humanity's course to one that respects Earth's systems, is Christiana Figueres, Costa Rican UN climate diplomat and orchestrator of the 2015 Paris Climate Accords. In an *OnBeing* podcast with Krista Tippett,[58] Figueres speaks to the need to claim joy as fuel for the hard work ahead of meeting 2030 goals to mitigate the worst climate eventualities. She also speaks of the need for *muscular hope,* how in this critical decade we must overcome fear-induced "paralysis" and continue to strengthen ourselves in ways of interconnection and solidarity. This too syncs with Sagittarius, whose totem is the centaur, with the chest and head of a human, and the body of a horse—which comes with strong legs!

While admitting to phases of very deep grief in her own life, particularly ecological grief, Christiana persists in returning to a mindset of presence and optimism. (Sagittarius /Jupiter has a reputation for magnetizing good fortune due to its attitude of optimism.) She refers to another conversation she's had, with writer Rebecca Solnit (author of *Hope In the Dark*, among many other books)) and Buddhist Roshi Joan Halifax, on the topic, "Uncertainty and Possibility: Meeting the Climate Future."[59] Caring for and focusing on the future, with a spiritually-tuned vision, these three powerful women set themselves to the task in a deeply thoughtful way.

In considering ourselves as the planet's future ancestors, they address the urgent need for a New Story (storytelling being Jupiter's domain par excellence.) A story that includes possibility, and collaboration with all beings. As part of this, they urge that we learn to train our thoughts and attention not on anxiety over what's failing and what's being lost, but on what is coming alive, and on what is noble and beautiful. There is in truth much to celebrate in this time.

Celebrations of the Light

In this season of darkness, Sagittarius also partakes of the essential practice of celebration. In pre-Christian times, the winter solstice was the marker for revelry. Here at this shortest day, when the visible light in the northern hemisphere ebbs to its lowest, the light begins to return. "Solstice," derived from the Latin *solstitium*, means "sun stands still." After months of becoming shorter and lower since the summer solstice, the Sun's arc through the sky comes to a rest, with it seeming to rise and set in the same two places for several days.

In the weeks surrounding this 'still point,' we are invited to a deepened companionship with darkness. Yet this is also a time when we celebrate and call on the Light by putting up lights, lighting candles, warming our hearts with uplifting music and, of equal import, turning towards the light within.

In Ancient Rome the *Saturnalia* winter solstice festival took place from December 17-24, in honor of Saturn who, prior to the birth of his son Jupiter (aka Zeus to the Greeks) was father of the gods. Suspending the usual discipline and order of Saturn's rule, a week of feasting and revelry ensued during the festival. Astrologers suggest that Jesus was a Pisces, not a Capricorn, as his Christmas birthdate implies. A pagan affirmation of this is that Jesus's December birthdate was selected by the Christians to offset the 'unleashed' *Saturnalia* celebrations; and in so doing, add a Christian significance to the solstice festivals so that church leaders could lure pagans to their cause.

Despite the church's possible co-opting, Christmas has been referred to as Yule, which may have been derived from the Norse word *jól*, referring to the solstice celebration. In

Scandinavia, the *Feast of Juul* was observed in pre-Christian times around the winter solstice. Fires were lit to signify the heat, light, and life-giving qualities of the returning Sun. A Yule, or Juul, log was brought in to burn on the hearth in honor of the Norse god Thor, counterpart to Jupiter.

Astrological gods of the season

I find it interesting that the earth festivals and zodiacal correlations of this season involve both Jupiter and Saturn, the two 'gateway' or 'social' planets who mediate between the fast-moving inner, 'personal' planets—Mercury, Mars, and Venus—and the slow-moving, outer, 'transpersonal' planets—Uranus, Pluto, and Neptune. Jupiter and Saturn (ruler of Capricorn, next up in the wheel) are the last two visible planets in the sky (Saturn being the furthest), and as such, beckon us toward worlds beyond visible sight—to the 'lights' we cannot see.

Though serving similar roles—helping us navigate with the larger social and transpersonal realms—the energies these two planets represent are seeming opposites, with Jupiter known for joyous optimism and expansion, and Saturn associated with caution, discipline, and privation. I find that one of the keys to grounding meaning in our own lives involves the artful integration of these two contrary impulses.

The anxious, constricted mindset of Saturn needs the uplift of Jupiter's faith and positivity. Jupiter invites us to look at what comes to us (or what doesn't come) as *gift*, rather than worrying about what might come to pass, or mourning what is no longer, or has not been. But if the world were all Centaur and no Goat (Capricorn's totem), we'd be bogged down by our ungrounded excesses, and foiled by unplanned or careless overshoots. As in all things Earth and Sky, balance is essential.

Reflected stained glass window lights at St. Michael's Church,
East Coker, where T.S. Eliot interred

The light we cannot see

I recently watched a gripping Netflix series, *All the Light We Cannot See*, based on the acclaimed book by Anthony Doerr. The title phrase alludes to words spoken by one of the story's characters, a French shortwave radio broadcaster during World War II, who called himself 'the professor' (a fitting Sagittarius archetype). His broadcast words were encoded messages for the Resistance forces, and at their surface meaning also offered a lifeline of wisdom and hope to the story's two other key protagonists, one of them a blind girl. "All the light we cannot see," a phrase the broadcaster used, speaks to the light within, the light of vision and imagination, which can inspire through a darkened time.

Exemplifying a nuanced understanding of the potential of Sagittarius, nature writer Annie Dillard[60] points out that the truth— the Light—cannot actually be 'found' or 'claimed', but only aimed at. For it is grace that bestows it. And, it is the pursuit—the journey itself—that offers a mighty fire of an engine to fuel our lives, particularly in troubled times.

> *The secret of seeing is…the pearl of great price…But although the pearl may be found, it may not be sought…although it comes to those who wait for it, it is always, even to the most practiced and adept, a gift and a total surprise…I cannot cause light; the most I can do is try to put myself in the path of its beam.*

Among the peaks

Sagittarius is the archetypal journeyer in quest of renewed vision, and under its sway we might feel called to don our pilgrim's robes. Travel, a strong Sagittarian pursuit, whether inner—through the world of higher meaning—or outer, to lofty mountaintops, is the means by which we can gain new perspectives, and thereby experience a revitalizing understanding for our lives. Into my inbox today dropped one such tale of a man's awakening,[61] literally amidst the Himalayan peaks, in which he gained new perspective through the complete cessation of thinking. (Hard for the busy Virgo mind to imagine!)

But as teacher and visionary Richard

Rocky peaks surround Santa Maria Abbey, Montserrat, Spain, pilgrimage spot hosting the Virgin of Montserrat Black Madonna

Rudd advises, we must be wary not to succumb to Sagittarius's ceaseless striving towards 'peak experiences.' Awakening can and often must happen within the ordinary. Travel to the planet's natural wonders and rare beauties compels most of us at one point or another, but really, any focused time spent in nature (which includes our own bodies as well as our local parks) can serve as an enchantment. As teacher/mythologist Michael Meade said in a recent talk, "For the Ancient Ones, nature was the holy with a green garment on, so it's a pilgrimage to go there. It's a 'divine errand.'"

Sometimes the Holy One's garment is flame red

The sage within

One of the wonderful gifts of being outdoors in presence with the earth, whatever the season or weather, is that it brings us into the moment, and calms our thoughts. Beauty, of course is one of Earth's great healing generosities. Writer/philosopher John O'Donohue suggests that beauty is God itself. Along the Sagittarius theme, he writes of the need for accessing our sage voice within, one that I feel can help guide us through these times of dissolution.

[This] voice whispers from somewhere beyond and encourages the human heart to hold out with dignity, respect, beauty, and human love. That whisper brings forgotten nobility into an arena where violence has traduced everything...This is the voice that keeps us directly in contact with the unalienable presence of beauty in the soul. Regardless of all the disappointments in life, this voice always remains to be heard deep within us. [62]

Indigenous Aleut elder Ilarion Merculieff, in a series of potent conversations with social activist Shariff Abdullah[63], stresses the same theme, that the way forward requires dropping into our hearts. To get there, he stresses, we must heal our traumas—only then can we stop the mind.

Right now the mind, which is the center of ego, wants to talk so much, because it's afraid it's going to die with our new direction. It'll keep on chattering—it always lives in the past, [considering] shame, remorse, rage, jealousy or fear, or a projecting of something into the future that hasn't happened yet. We're being called to come to the Now. Because in the present moment there is no Time...The answers we need as to what to do are in our hearts.

Further expanding this perspective, through a lens of Sagittarian optimism that stands against the prevalent sense of doom, Shariff Abdullah urges us to consider the disruptions of our time as that of a birth (which he points out is often in itself a process of messy upheaval):

The problems that we now have are the trigger points that spur us to a new society. The things we label as "the problem," are really only what gets us to a new society. These are the points of birth, [signaling] that we're about to be born into something. This is the point where we hit metamorphosis.

Navigating the sea of (mis)information

A post-US election (November 2024) opinion piece in my local newspaper described how the author was done believing in the 'bubble' of the Democrat-leaning, corporate-ruled, media machine, and determined to take back his time—to go fishing, and to reengage with other hands-on pursuits. There is wisdom in this impulse to take back our life from domination by the media swamp.

But it's not so easy. We are now deeply entrained in the too-frequent habit of informing ourselves about the undoing of the status quo; yet we are also in an astrological time where important insights and revelations are available *through* the wires of communication, with Uranus the awakener in Gemini for the most part until 2032 (except for the first 3.5 months of 2026, when it retrogrades to Taurus). While curious Gemini checks out any and all information and gossip without discrimination, it needs Sagittarius to help frame what it is we're looking for, so that Uranus can do its job of lifting up our consciousness!

The shift to a strong Air sign signature now in play, with Pluto in Aquarius and Uranus in Gemini, will continue to compel us to engage with the mind and the realm of ideas, and ideally in ways that offer new perspectives that our authentic self resonates with. Questioning old ways of thinking, and gently exploring the ideas of others not necessarily part of one's 'tribe', is a good start! Sagittarius can benefit from this nudge to question its typically judgmental stance on things.

Suspend

A word that has been coming to me recently is one my husband used to use years ago when contemplating the works of theoretical physicist David Bohm. "Suspend!" he used to interject at times, invoking Bohm's philosophical lynchpin of 'suspending assumptions' mid-conversation. The word feels to me the right medicine for our time, as the warring, 'othering' attitude of left vs. right, righteous vs. pernicious, continues to fly out of hand. What if every time we catch our thoughts cycling in a fear—or othering—space, we stop, breathe, and suspend?

I found a YouTube clip of Bohm[64] in which, for elevated 'clout', he sits beside the Dalai Lama, offering wise advice, more relevant now than ever. Bohm counsels that we listen deeply to the views of others, without resistance. "We cannot do this if we hold to our own opinion and resist the other," he says. This directly addresses the Sagittarian shadow tendency to push their ideas and beliefs on others as 'the only truth.'

One of the greatest obstacles to achieving open-minded dialogue in our era of mashable truths is that we so fiercely stand in our opinions—formed by cherished information sources, which routinely put down and distort the 'opposition's' truths and their media sources—that it becomes a major feat for those with opposing viewpoints to listen deeply to each other. Each comes with volumes of media intake supporting their beliefs. As Armenian mystic and spiritual teacher G.I. Gurdjieff said, "People can be made to believe any old tale, and frothing at the mouth will set themselves to convince others that it is so and cannot be otherwise."[65]

To this end, we may at times find ourselves in a cul de sac of exasperation when attempting open-minded exchange. But by broadening our perspective and opening our minds to other views, perhaps we can access the shift of consciousness that the time is moving us towards.

The mind-suspending spaciousness of a Scottish Highlands landscape

From belief to being

The Sagittarius archetype presides over belief systems and worldviews. But in an era where collapse is at hand, not just environmentally and politically, but also with systems of belief, people increasingly define themselves as "spiritual but not religious," or "political but not spiritual." I read recently that technocrat Peter Thiel defines himself as "religious but not spiritual," so there's that too! Belief is becoming increasingly divisive. Maybe here too, we need a reframe.

Richard Rudd[66] discusses the necessity of moving from the victim mindset to a freedom mindset—freedom being an appealing ideal for both Sagittarius and Aquarius. Rudd suggests that spiritual seeking itself (a Sagittarius clarion call) can unwittingly lure us into a victim mentality, in that it makes us feel we have to *do* something (practice more, better!) in order to find fulfillment in some other, unobtainable reality than the one with shadows and emotional pain that we may know.

"If you create an unattainable reality, then you can spend your whole life longing for that reality without ever having to directly experience it," he says. This encapsulates the restless Sagittarius dilemma of being attached to the quest, without ever settling in to embody the treasure and be transformed by it.

Rudd proposes that an 'enlightenment experience' isn't really what we're after, being that awakening resides in the ordinary. "In fact," he says, "high levels of frequency tear down the very illusion that there is such a thing as *spiritual* experience…True freedom has nothing to do with how we spend our time on the material plane. True freedom is not an effect. It is a kind of ever-expanding spaciousness that arises spontaneously inside you as you come to understand how deeply victimized you really are by your own core beliefs."

The mystical 13th c. Persian poet[67], Rumi, concurs:

This is how people live. Sleeping on the banks of a fresh water stream, but with their lips always dry with thirst. In your dream you're running towards a mirage. And as you run, you're proud of being the one who sees a false oasis. You brag about it to your friends. "Look, I have the heart vision!" But listen, this love of spying what's far off keeps you from tasting the real water of where and who you are now. The real way is who and where you already are. What you search for is sleeping in your very being. And that which sleeps and dreams of sweet water is the taste of the divine in you.

The joy in gratitude

Imagine if we could experience this sense of spaciousness Rudd speaks of around all the *what ifs* we now attach our thinking to, around the fears of having our notions of fairness and respect crushed, or around the very real losses and challenges we have or are ongoingly experiencing.

When we can reach a place of inner spaciousness, the Sagittarian gift of intuition is most likely to be engaged. And it is the intuitions of the heart that will serve as our navigation system through the chaotic waters of the times ahead. Such direct knowing is not mediated by the head, but from full-bodied experiencing, such as we find in breathwork, movement practices, and other forms of mindful presence…like fishing!

The 'truth' that Sagittarius is after, in the end, is not a set of teachings we encounter or a summit we ascend, but something we come to know in our Being. It is achieved by facing the inner truth of our Scorpionic suffering, adventuring through the systems of thought and foreign terrain that this noble Fire sign impels us to, and coming back home (like Ulysses).

It is not joy that makes us grateful; it is gratitude that makes us joyful
~ Brother David Steindl-Rast

Minding the Interior: Capricorn

~ December 21-January 20

In the point of rest at the center of our being, we encounter a world where all things are at rest in the same way. Then a tree becomes a mystery, a cloud a revelation, each [person] a cosmos of whose riches we can only catch glimpses. The life of simplicity is simple, but it opens to us a book in which we never get beyond the first syllable.

~ Dag Hammarskjöld[68]

Greetings from the still, quiet center of Capricorn's issue, opening at the point of longest night—the winter solstice, when the seed of light is planted in the deep dark, initiating a period of rest while we await Light's return. Whether outwardly or within, the Capricorn phase can feel a long ordeal, a journey through thick time, which one must patiently endure before the gears of the year start their motion.

Fittingly, patience is one of the primary qualities to which Capricorn, and its ruler Saturn, apprentices us. When we submit to the task, waiting with attentive openness for the dormant to arise, keeping the inward gaze that this yin sign invites, we can meet this Wise Guardian energy with all of ourselves and, with grace, reap its rewards come spring.

This season of darkest days begins with heightened energies. Ushered in by the spark of music, the lighting of lights, and festive adornments, whether for solstice or religious holidays, we come together for rituals with family or community. Yet for some, these times are charged—be it with longing for connections that are no more, or perhaps never were.

Those with a natal chart imprint of Saturn, Capricorn's ruler, in relationship with the Moon (or Cancer) may instead feel called inward, away from the thrum, perhaps into deeper connection with Capricorn's Earth element, or its mystical side—seeking a light or quality of communion through beauty and/or the natural world that family may not provide.

Dual nature: the goat-fish

Signified in modern times by the mountain goat—wanderer of icy heights, comfortable in cold and challenging conditions—Capricorn in its esoteric origins bears the mark of the reclusive Hermit/Seer, primed to bear the harshness of solitude and rugged conditions in its quest to birth the light within. This impulse is echoed by the outer story of the rebirth of the light, as well as the story of the birth of Jesus, calendared during Capricorn's time.

With its lofty aspirations, Capricorn leads us into the fourth quadrant of zodiac signs, of those that preside over big-picture matters, perspectives, and sensibilities. Yet the archetype is also grounded in and beholden to what we call reality—to material plane limits and obligations. The sign's duality is signified by its original totem as the mythical goat with a fish's tail, indicating the archetype's capacity to navigate subterranean waters, as well as rocky peaks. So while the Capricorn archetype in our time is known as the maintainer of traditions and structures, and thereby associated with patriarchal masculine energy, as an Earth sign connected with the waters of origin, it is in fact Feminine.

Considering the meaning of its month, January, derived from *Janus*, reenforces this duality. *Janus* was an Ancient Roman god of doorways and beginnings who, presiding over transitions, was often depicted with two bearded heads facing opposite directions—hence the phrase, *Janus-faced*, which points to the *capri-cious,* or contradictory, nature of the god.

Indeed, Capricorn commands the heights of worldly realms, where it strives with ambition and disciplined know-how toward the top of the corporate or societal ladder, while also bearing the potential to access the deepest mystical knowing. Whatever it strives after, in its noblest sense the endeavor it pits its energies towards is founded on a deep self-respect, with a 'mountain mind' unshakeable in pursuit of its goals.

While known for its leadership qualities, as a humble Earth sign, Capricorn is also 'salt of the earth'—determinedly hard working, and not afraid to roll up its sleeves and participate. Often a solitary journeyer, however, Capricorn, and its ruler Saturn, can invite the trials of loneliness (it's lonely at the top!). But as astrologer Daniel Giamario points out, genuine personal evolution and soul growth take place only within the individual, not the collective. This is why inner work is so vital in these times, as true change in the collective begins with each of us.

Steadfast she goes

On my walks of late I have been captivated by the simple beauty of the few remaining golden oak tree leaves clinging determinedly to their branches—perhaps an original inspiration for tree ornaments! As well, I've noted a marked increase in front yards adorned not just with lights, but with trees trimmed with bulb ornaments— proliferating like (upside down) mushrooms! As well, there's a growing trend towards deer sculptures, fitting given that the deer is another Capricorn totem! Perhaps there is afoot a subconscious harkening back towards pagan origins, when the trees and animals themselves were seen and respected as holy.

A graceful temple—refugia

I've been struck this season by the de-emphasis of the Christmas/Christian story and themes, both within and around me. On Christmas Day on a walk at the Sonoma Coast, only one person from among many that we passed offered up a "Merry Christmas!" Indicators suggest we may have at last set sail onto the sea of new myth-making, with the earth as principal dream-weaver—as it must be if we are to survive as a planet and species.

I see the 'remainder' oak tree leaves as emblems of *refugia*, an ecological term used to denote an environment that has proven resilient to ecological change and is hence able to offer habitat for that which is endangered. The capacity to hold on under duress and provide for others, through its gift of steadfastness, is decidedly Capricornian, for this archetype presides over and excels at the building or curating of lasting systems. At a time when the traditional structures of our Western world are undeniably toppling, as is the homeostasis of the planet's ecological systems, we need *refugia* beacons.

Nobles among us

As the deciduous trees surrender their spent leaves to the waiting earth below, yielding a new landscape of branches bared to sky, my attention has been called to the evergreens—the mighty redwoods, the cedars, the pines—whose aspiring erectness rises skyward without meandering. Not distracted by the horizontal plane of life, or the coming and going of leaves, the evergreens are called into the heights of sky, not unlike Capricorn, who specializes in filtering out inessentials in order to achieve its goals. As I contemplate the pointed peaks of the evergreens, my mind flies to the mountains of the California Sierra, where the eye can travel along vast swaths of steep mountainsides laden with colonies of these upward-rising nobles.

Unlike trees, the notion of a 'noble class' among humans, as seen through the eye awakened to social justice, is clearly a dying order, one based in hierarchy, wealth, and privilege afforded by birth. Pluto's 16-year tenure in Capricorn brought first the exposure of our structures' corruption, and then its steady unraveling, accelerated by the pandemic. As it has crumbled, technocrats, themselves operating like bacteria and viruses, have become embedded in our systems—unscrupulous outsiders not part of the dying Capricornian old-world, ruling elites. Whatever industry they pander to, and wherever they spring from, those in charge are driven by greed, equipped with billions, and have grabbed power in corporate and political spheres.

As I've said, despite this, I and those I trust take the long view in the face of the collapse of once-trusted institutions and systems, whether human-made, or of Earth herself. Facing our grief over what is falling and has been lost is necessary, but equally so are individual efforts to focus on and offer the sustenance and light of solidarity, to serve as progenitors of a new (Aquarian) way of life. This may sound like fantasy, but it is founded in an understanding of the cycles of time, of death and rebirth, and of the not yet tapped power of the human being to harness its highest capacities towards transformation.

Out with the old?

There has been much talk about Pluto's transition from Capricorn into Aquarius, where it resides from 2025-2043. The 'death and transformation' planet's time in idealistic Aquarius is already reflecting sweeping changes across the collective. Whereas Capricorn's means are in building enduring institutions and protocols, Aquarius the revolutionary is keen to break these down, to level the playing field so that a new vision can take root. (The French Revolution took place in the latter part of a Pluto run through Aquarius.)

It was fitting that during the Capricorn moment of old structures crumbling, Netflix put up its final season of *The Crown*. In its final episode, Queen Elizabeth contemplates her death, and questions the monarchy's ensuing viability. Prince Philip utters these apposite words:

The system makes no sense anymore to those outside it, nor to those of us inside it. All human things are subject to decay, and when fate summons, even monarchs must obey…

This is indeed the Capricornian predicament. While a master builder of empire, subject as all things are to the cycles of life, empire is destined to decay. Civilizations as well. Depth psychological and visionary astrologer, Dane Rudhyar, wrote presciently:

Civilization—the Capricornian god—must forever destroy itself while increasing its scope and its powers. Its noblest children are the very ones who will be the leaders in this destruction: the reformers and dreamers, these minds whom no achievement can ever satisfy. They will carry in their souls the signature of Aquarius.[69]

Of course, it's not a linear 'out with the old, in with the new' process, but more of a spiral. With Saturn as traditional ruler (and Uranus as modern ruler), Aquarius, like Capricorn, has strong "power over" impulses, which we see in spades in today's world. The worst-case scenario for Pluto in Aquarius is a world ever more dominated by despots, with the media and AI as primary weapons of control—technological innovations being governed by Uranus. Thus empowered, fearsome con men disguised as rulers lure the people into entrusting them with their will, and surrendering responsibility to them for their lives.

Lumen Natura

Rather than dwell on the perceived dark, however, I take my cue from the sprouting seed, which tunes its growth towards the sun's warmth, even while initially buried in the dark. It is not "Pollyanna" to look to what is good, beautiful, and burgeoning in a time of dying. To this end, I am keen to elevate Capricorn's crusty reputation and find the light of hope therein, a light that springs both from its earthy practicality and its esoteric knowledge of the Mystery.

We have Claudius Ptolemy, 2nd century Egyptian astronomer and astrologer to thank for condensing down the Capricorn signification to mere masculine means and methods, tossing out the internal, mystical qualities inherent in the sign. But there are those of us astrologers determined to restore Capricorn's spiritual signification. Rudhyar, in pointing to Capricorn's arrival at the inception of the return of the light in the earth's yearly orbit around the Sun, describes this sign's essence as the initiation of the growing "Day Force," which will peak at the summer solstice. He equates this Day-Force with what he calls "the Christos," the birth of the Christ, which marks a "descent of Spirit into matter."

Other, pagan-leaning sources suggest that Capricorn represents the hidden seed of mystical light that is found in nature (the *lumen natura*), given its associations with the nature god, Pan, and its being the most 'big picture' of the practical Earth signs, with an inherent concern for the systems of the natural world. The Ancient Greek and Hindu gods associated with Capricorn presided over agriculture, and the essential rains that nourished the crops. As protectors of the land, which in ancient times was essential for survival, these gods understood and worked to maintain the interconnected web of earthly life.

'Protector' is a key aspect of Capricorn leadership. And as such, at its most elevated, this archetype takes responsibility for sustaining the delicate web of life on Earth, using its intuitive connection to the earth's denizens, elements, and cycles, along with its forward-looking, wise elder view, to make sure that Life will continue to thrive for seven generations to come.

The eyes of the future are looking back at us.
And they are praying for us to see beyond our own time.
~ Terry Tempest Williams

Alchemical opus: the Nigredo

The Capricorn archetype, in its integrity, propels us to 'take care of business,' and to focus on bringing our best selves forward in our social interfaces. The qualities of its polarity partner, Cancer—tending, caring, and holding—are mostly absent in today's public arenas, and need to be resurrected in social realms. It is and will continue to be up to us, in our individual lives, to bring these soul-sustaining qualities back into 'convention', during what will likely be a challenging time of transition, termed by depth psychologist Francis Weller as "the long dark."

Capricorn is the archetype that opens out into this long wait for redemption, at times through darkness and despair. As such, Capricorn/Saturn can be associated with depression, and a profound loss of hope. Alchemically, Saturn is associated with the *nigredo,* meaning blackness, symbolized by the raven. Phases or encounters with the *nigredo* become known to us as deep disappointment, dullness, or feelings of alienation from ourselves or others.

This blackness or "lead" is the alchemical *prima materia* through which we must work on our shadow, in Jungian terms. Saturn represents the base metal that must be cooked until it emits a putrid aroma. This is the precursor of the release of 'spirit' that forms the Philosopher's Stone (aka the gold). If successful, the shadow is released, so that it can wither and fall, like leaves from a tree, allowing us to grow beyond obsolete and harmful ways.

This Saturnian process of 'coagulation' or extraction of the lead within, is associated with death, hence the potential for certain Saturn aspects in a chart natally and by transit to coincide with difficult times, whether physically or emotionally. Steadfastness and patience are the necessary medium of the undertaking. The staying power to wait through a winter of isolation and bleakness, to endure the wasteland, to surrender to the process of letting go of what needs to 'die,' is a hidden gift of the mature Capricorn.

The process is quickened by the Feminine capacity to dissolve rigidity by going within, accepting what is present, or empty, and engaging with some form of imaginal shape shifting. All of this is on offer with the energy of transiting Saturn conjunct Neptune (see below), operative to varying degrees until 2027. With these two energies combined, we are called to sift and evaluate old habits of being and responding that have become second nature, and toss the ones that no longer belong. Those with weak boundaries (which Pisces/Neptune often indicates), are called to practice not giving more of ourselves than we have bandwidth for.

Death of the old king and queen

The heart of psycho-spiritual alchem-ical work, known as 'the union of the opposites,' involves joining our ego per-sona with our soul qualities, integrat-ing the best of masculine and feminine: Sun and Moon, strength and flexibil-ity, action and receptivity, doing and being. The potential for this resides in Capricorn's dual nature—its striving after spirit's peaks and spires, and its

King & Queen lying in state, Victoria & Albert Museum, London

groundedness in the knowledge of the earth and the waters of our origins. Astrology, also concerned with the integration of opposing energies, has been closely linked with alchemy by figures such as C.G. Jung—himself a Saturnian wise man figure, with Saturn in his 1st House and Capricorn co-ruling his Aquarius Ascendant. As previously noted, Jung was deeply engaged in studies of both astrology and alchemy.

Metaphorically, one could say that purifying the lead signifies the 'stinking despair' that alchemists suggested the withering part must go through, before it can be transmuted. Whether an individual, or a civilization, Saturn represents the 'old king and queen' who must die and be laid to rest, entombed in grief and isolation, subjected to long waiting, before the subsequent transformation is initiated from the depths. The process cannot be forced or precipitated through Will by the one going through it, but only tended from within with patience.

Shortly after writing the above, I encountered a quote by D.H. Lawrence for Epiphany, Jan. 6, in a Book of Days, which lands temporally with precision on this and other Capricorn themes.

> *Let me only be still, and know we can force nothing, and compel nothing, can only nourish in the darkness the unuttered buds of the new life that shall be. That is our life now: this nourishing of the germs the unknown quickens when the new life is coming into being in us and in others—only patience, only patience, and endless courage to reject false dead things and false, killing processes.*[70]

The attendant qualities of isolation and grief greatly inform our time, as well as the month of Capricorn, as the old slowly fades. These times and its inherent qualities must be tended to with great care, subtlety, and attention, not brushed aside or denied. For they are not without inner riches, Capricorn informs us. Faith in the mysterious workings of the unseen is key. Eventually, we meet up with change—who knows, maybe even the Philosopher's Stone!

Choosing Earth

As to the 'mundane life' quarter, where most of us spend the bulk of our time, Capricorn offers some sage advice on the importance, at this time of climate collapse, of "voluntary simplicity." Simple living, in awareness of the preciousness of natural resources, was instinctively practiced by Indigenous cultures, until 'civilized folk' took over and tried to re-educate them into their own mores and religions. This included the proposition of a transcendent male God that is separate from and 'lords over' the material plane realm, replacing the natural Feminine awareness that the Divine is immanent in all life and its processes.

Choosing Earth[71] is an important book by futurist Duane Elgin, which I read when it first came out in 2020, and subsequently facilitated book groups for. The book carefully illustrates the signs of 'climate collapse' that Elgin had foreseen since the 1980s when working to research and forecast the effects of climate change for the Stanford Research Institute. So as not to scare the bejesus out of us, he carefully refers to these as the 'Stages of Initiation and Transformation' (Capricorn is associated with initiatory rites of passage), and goes on to detail what he calls "Uplifts for a Transforming Future." Fear is ever the devil at the door in Saturn-land—one could say the primary alchemical 'lead' we must work with, along with despair. So the practice of facing our fears and funding the resolve to feel and move through them is paramount in the domain. Keeping tools of 'uplift' at our side is essential.

Alchemical gold

While Elgin does not shy away from telling us how he saw and sees it (he foresaw that the early 2020s would be when the unraveling would virulently begin), the real gold of the book is in the Uplifts section. Here he helps people face what is upon us with (Capricornian) maturity and realism, inviting us to dig into the work of preparing ourselves—mind, body, and spirit—to live creatively and joyfully into the challenges ahead.

Voluntary simplicity

Following on the "choosing" theme (inherent in Capricornian responsibility), Elgin includes multiple sections in the book that all begin with the word Choosing: Aliveness, Consciousness, Communication, Maturity, Reconciliation, Community, Simplicity, and Our Future.

All of these have great merit, but for present purposes I am highlighting Simplicity. This is something we can each concretely hold to—scaling back on the excesses of our lives, such as our acquisition and holding of material possessions, and our style of consuming natural resources (energy, water, food, plastics, textiles, etc.), in preparation and respect for a time when resources will be less abundant, as they were in centuries past.

I've been working on getting my body used to cooler indoor temps both day and night for the past two years, turning my thermostat down a couple of degrees through time. To my surprise, this year when I arise to 58° temps indoors, I no longer cringe at the cold, but instead feel beneficially 'braced! (A 'clothes-on' version of the cold water plunge?) We do need polarity sign Cancer's qualities to navigate successfully with Capricorn, however—this is not military rule!

For Cancerian comfort, I drink warm lemon water and hot teas, wear warm wraps over my sweaters, and cozy up with lap blankets in the evenings in winter. Part of my coming to enjoy cooler indoor temps derives, I believe, from having conviction in my intent, in the choice I'm making. Knowing as I do of natural gas' limited supply, as well as the harm to the waters and habitats that fracking induces, and its rising cost.

I know, this may come off as annoying (Virgo) 'virtue signaling,' but it is not meant so! I only mean to suggest that changing our lifestyle, while initially uncomfortable, can with time become new routine that is personally gratifying. Although, it's true that Capricorn happily embraces "austerity measures," such as the wild goat who navigates cold and steep inclines when scaling a peak. And I know this drill isn't for everyone. I confess to having natal Saturn *in* Capricorn, tightly opposing my Moon, so Saturn and I walk hand in hand through life!

The Saturn-Neptune project

As referenced in my Aries chapter and in this one, Saturn is conjunct Neptune in Aries until 2027. This is significant as it marks the start of a new Saturn-Neptune cycle, with the previous one initiated in 1989, at the break-up of the USSR. This time, the conjunction remarkably starts at 0° Aries, the Creator point of the zodiac. It unites the grounding capacities of Saturn with Neptunian dreams and visions, and the undercurrents of the collective—whether its delusions and denials, or the inspirations needed for seeding the future. As popular astrologer Pam Gregory dubs it, this is about "making real the dream."

Alas, we are plainly seeing the shadow potential of this combination, which is Neptunian insanity and disability overtaking the structures of governance and media. However, with the conjunction in the sign Aries, the conjunction bears the potential for mounting compassion-based actions, and the pioneering of initiatives that—in their highest manifestation—can harness transcendent capacities and creativity in service to societal change. This is a long-term process, so the medicine of patience will be much needed, along with faith.

While walking one evening this month during an intensely windy rainstorm, I was struck by the sight of a neon-lit, wire-fashioned snowman that had capsized. The image I vaguely saw in the rainy mist was of a giant platypus, swimming across the water-soaked grass. I flashed to a thought of a 'new world order,' a watery one, where the Feminine prevails, in which the symbols that once stood stately and erect (and happy, as snowmen will be—or used to be, before global warming!), have fallen, and are now swimming in waterways close to the earth. Perhaps this was an emanation in anticipation of this new Saturn-Neptune cycle!

Response-ability

Increasingly, I return to Capricorn/ Saturn's chief medicine: that of learning to set limits and boundaries, and of taking responsibility for our part in things. These are the keys to claiming our true maturity, and to mastering the planetary transits

as well! Alluded to above, some of the most fruitful applications of claiming responsibility in our lives are in relationships.

Relevant to co-dependent dynamics, when we seek to help or rescue others (often funded by the Pisces/Neptune impulse), we unwittingly deny them the chance to learn to take responsibility for themselves, making them reliant on us. But when we refrain from getting overly involved, we free others to take charge of themselves. A perfect example of this was reported in the *Sebastopol Times* online news, in an article about a local facility for the homeless called *Horizon Shine*, quoting someone who used to be homeless herself.

> *Mistry Lujan, the case manager at Horizon Shine, said, "I've been where [the clients] are at currently; I've been there and I got through it. And I didn't get through it with services of any kind, but **I had the chance to actually navigate myself through it**. [my emphasis] And so I love the chance to empower anybody to move forward with their life."*

This is what Capricorn/Saturn calls for, that we learn to empower ourselves by taking responsibility for our own needs and circumstances. We don't make others responsible for us or blame them, and we don't go overboard helping others do what they feasibly can do for themselves. We also refrain from victim stance, from attributing our challenges and misfortunes to outside agents or forces. Instead, we take action to improve things. This is real maturity, the centered embodiment of Capricorn.

Ethics of reciprocity

An aspect of owning our human responsibility as stewards of the earth is through practicing reciprocity. In an interview about her book, *The Serviceberry*, scientist and Indigenous teacher Robin Wall Kimmerer[72] (author of *Braiding Sweetgrass*) touches on the idea of balanced give and take. As a corollary to the foundational Indigenous practice of reciprocity with the earth—of giving back whenever one takes while harvesting, of taking only what one needs, and never more than half—she points to the need for us to give our gifts to society.

> *When someone gives you a gift, you want to give them something. You are in their debt, in a way, and you want to honor them and respect them in the way that you've been respected. And so that opens the door to reciprocity, to say, well, what is the gift that*

I could give you in return for water or berries or birdsong. . .? And that requires that deep self-examination to say, well, what is my gift? And which of my gifts are what the world needs in this moment? And now we're talking about a purpose-driven life, right? To say... I matter too. My participation, my gifts, need to be in the world in order for the world to thrive.

Another element of a thriving world that Kimmerer emphasizes is 'enoughness', relevant to the idea of the 'ethical harvest', which considers all the other beings that benefit from a plant offering when one is 'taking'. She writes in *Braiding Sweetgrass* how gratitude for what we have creates an experience of fullness, whereas ours is an economy fueled by the notion of emptiness. "The notion of gratitude, enoughness, and abundance feel so important as an antidote to the endless need to consume," she says.

The idea of having enough, of being content with what we have, jibes well with the traditional Capricornian values of frugality and respect for the earth's limited natural resources. Yet Capricorn in modern times has run amok with the concept of success defined as abundance and continuous acquisition. Depth psychologist James Hillman suggests that "the harvest has become the hoard...The ripened end-product and in-gathering...under the aegis of Saturn can show qualities of greed and tyranny, where in-gathering means holding and the pursuit of miserliness, making things last through all time."[73]

The impulse to 'conserve' based on understanding the finite limits of what the earth offers has morphed into an amassing and hoarding instinct. When this is practiced to the excess that it now is, the necessary flow of energy (whether of money, or of other resources like food and water) becomes stifled, leading ultimately to systems failure. Releasing acquired wealth and energy back into the system, whether through philanthropy or 'spending down', requires trusting that what goes around comes around, that all life is interconnected and thrives together, that oneself and one's family alone is not the best final destination of assets accrued.

This rethinking and redistribution of riches in such a way that dissolves greed and releases the fear of lack is another area of potential change that this new Saturn-Neptune cycle, supported by the systems-thinking potential of Pluto in Aquarius, may provoke. May we all do our part in the necessary rebalancing of resource use, and earth stewardship, as mature Capricorn protectors.

11

WHEELS OF CHANGE: AQUARIUS
~ January 21-February 18

Antonio Gaudi's innovative wheel motifs at Casa Batlló, Barcelona

You are something the whole universe is doing in the same way that a wave is something that the whole ocean is doing.
~Alan Watts

Moving through the astrological and seasonal cycles that hold us, we arrive now at change-able Aquarius, which begins at mid-winter in the Gregorian calendar, while also announc-ing the beginning of spring in pagan and Chinese traditions. Given this sign's inherent duality, it is fittingly a phase and an energy of both continued limitation—of cold, and stillness—and of rebirth's first awakening, such as we find in the form of soft pink plum blossoms here in the north.

With Saturn as its traditional ruler, when the Sun passes through Aquarius we may experience the energy of *continued* internalization, given that Saturn ruled prior sign, Capricorn, as well. But detached Air sign Aquarius is perhaps better known for its outgoing, open-minded, and freedom-loving perspective on life, reflecting its modern ruler, Uranus. The sign's dual rulership describes its paradoxes: for it is both rebellious and unpredictable (Uranus), and determined and disciplined (Saturn). When these divergent facets are integrated, the essence of the archetype serves as a catalyst of inspired innovation, and a weaver of higher truths through inspiring words and grounded actions. At its heart, Aquarius serves change.

Aquarian work is universal work, as alluded to above by Alan Watts, reflecting on how the work of the individual is to serve the Whole. This reflects the notion of the 'holographic paradigm', which I first encountered in the mid-1980s upon moving to California from the East Coast, in the popular book, *The Aquarian Conspiracy,* by Marilyn Ferguson. The holographic paradigm refers to the interconnectedness of all existence, how the whole is reflected within each part. The entire web of life, including consciousness and the invisible realms, is of a piece. From this perspective, everything affects everything else, including material plane existence.

Writer, Trappist monk, and mystic Thomas Merton—whose Sun, Mars, Mercury, Jupiter, Uranus, and North Node were *all* in Aquarius—beautifully exemplifies Aquarius' wide-seeing consciousness, as well as its reclusive tendencies. While living in retreat from ordinary life, Merton contributed greatly to the ideas of the time, both politically and spiritually, through his many writings. He wrote:

My job is to press forward, to grow interiorly, to pray, to break away from attachments and to defy fears; to grow in faith, which has its own solitude, to see an entirely new perspective and new dimensions in my life. To open up new horizons at any cost.[74]

Overcoming (Saturnian) fears, breaking from attachments, and pursing new horizons (Uranus)—these reflect a truly Aquarian approach to life. Like the previous sign, Capricorn, Aquarius is linked with two elements. While a social Air sign, it is known symbolically as "the water-bearer" for its association with the universal 'font of knowledge'. To access these waters of wisdom, Aquarius calls on the capacity of the mind to 'download' information from other realms, as well as to synthesize and combine ideas in new ways, and with new perspectives.

Merton embodied both the spiritual knowing, and the devotion of the Water element, and a detached, mental genius that witnessed the course of the world and wrote copiously about it. Sadly, he died unexpectedly, by electrocution—a truly Uranian way to go! (Uranus ruling electricity, shock, and 'aha' moments.)

Tension of the Opposites: Self vs. Community

Merton's book, *Thoughts in Solitude*, is aptly named, given that Aquarius, while aspiring to Unity, also carries the torch for personal individuation as separate and apart from the group, due to its Uranus influence. To achieve an authentic, separate identity, solitude is necessary. One cannot individuate, or easily innovate, from within a group. Here is a central paradox of Aquarius—it is determined to live for and embrace the collective, and yet it urges us to develop our uniqueness.

It seems to me that this tension between wanting to contribute to society, to be part of something—whether a movement, a team, a cause, or a community—and wanting to be alone, in order to connect with oneself and the vast more-than-human world that exists beyond the self, whether that of nature and the stars, or other planes of existence and ways of knowing, will be baked into the years ahead, with Pluto now concentrated through the Aquarian theme until 2043. The Pluto 'game' of transformation, if you will, will be an Aquarian one. Intentional time taken in solitude will be needed in order to deprogram ourselves from centuries of Capricornian and Piscean (see below on Piscean era) conditioning. But coming *out* of isolation, a disease of our time, and joining our essential selves with community, will be an equally vibrant theme. The collective needs individuated selves! Individuals need to express in the collective!

Aquarius works in tandem with its polarity partner, Leo. Finding release from our acculturated beliefs and ways in part requires coming down off the ego-obsession of distorted Leo energy. Exaggerated self-focus and self-aggrandizement is another sickness of our time, necessitating the antidote of the Aquarian vision of all beings as equally special. We need to achieve the Goldilocks effect here—finding just enough ego to make an authentic, creative contribution, while offering it in service to a shared vision that welcomes and honors the greater community of Life.

Barcelona shop honors the greater community (including the giraffe)

Of rights and rites

In honor of this idea of universal inclusivity, German-born British composer Max Richter and his ensemble created a hauntingly beautiful piece, *Voices* (2020), featuring readings from the Universal Declaration of Human Rights, which was adopted by the UN General Assembly in December 1948, with Eleanor Roosevelt serving as chair of the drafting committee. It is a great irony that this was the very year of the *Nakba*, the war on Palestine, and its resulting expulsion of Palestinians from their homeland. We are surely at a planetary low point in the honoring of human rights, with much work yet ahead. Perhaps the regression in this area now will seed a powerful movement to right current wrongs.

Turning to the other-than-human community, I have been learning about African elephant tribes and their behaviors through the graceful work of writer and conservationist, Eleanor O'Hanlon[75], who travels to and shares about some of the world's oldest and wisest animal beings. The mores of the ancient elephants provide a powerful window into the integrated Aquarian-Leo polarity, given that they are very social animals—even democratic (!), allowing anyone—even the young—to at times influence the elder leaders' decisions, while also conveying an enormous amount of Leonine love to their family members. This love is lavished upon the infants, through the touch and play offered by many elders, as well as on the deceased, for whom continued reverence is shown both in memory and in actions. (Elephants spend sometimes weeks standing beside the boney remains of their dead.)

In Aquarian fashion, elephants' seeing stretches beyond the now, into deep time, picking up on the vibrations of their ancestors. We might take them as a model in reclaiming the wisdom of our own ancestors, honoring their suffering, as well as the value of the lived experiences of our own personal past. In our post-modern 'screen era', excessively mental Aquarius energy—isolated, detached, and often overly captured by futuristic visions (such as the virtual world of Mark Zuckerberg's *Meta*, and Jeff Bezos' outer space exploits)—risks forgetting that love and passion are the anchors of earthly life. Bringing in the heart center, and playful camaraderie, as elephants and other animals know to do, is key.

Other ways of knowing: tuning in vs. tampering

Elephants also appear to be remarkably connected to the geomagnetic lines within the earth, which it is suggested help them know how to source water sometimes hundreds of miles away. This echoes Aquarius' association with geomagnetic, as well as electrical, waves as sources of intelligence, and brings to mind the astonishing power of winged ones like butterflies and sand hill cranes to navigate thousands of miles back to where their parents had come from. Aquarius is the significator of technology, which many other life forms besides humans have mastered.

Perhaps this 'tuning in' to felt sense knowing that these other-than-human beings excel at is a capacity that, in this Aquarian era, we can look to re-cultivate within ourselves, and which members of Indigenous nations still hold. With 'higher mind' Uranus now in open-minded Gemini for the most part until 2033, and Uranus in an ongoing triangle formation (supporting higher-level change) with Pluto and Neptune until 2028, achieving this is indeed possible.

Along these (electrical) lines, on a more cautionary note, astrologer Mark Jones, in an *Astrology University* webinar on Pluto in Aquarius, cites an article stating that 5G and 6G wireless cellular network technology can potentially degrade the accuracy of weather forecasts by as much as 30%, as it disrupts necessary water vapor signals. These signals are sensitive to 'noise' near the ground, and when disrupted, diminish the capacities of satellites to measure them. Inaccurate weather reports do not bode well for food harvests Sadly, too, birds, as well as bees and other insects, are affected by electromagnetic radiation[76]. It is suggested that it is contributing to bee population die-off.

The human flaw, or trauma signature

Connecting to our non-human kin can help us connect back to our own essence, which is the process of individuation that Uranus calls us to. But this is delicate work. In his book, *Healing the Soul,* Mark Jones discusses how the unique "genius" within, signified by Uranus, is often entangled within a trauma signature. As the higher octave of Mercury, Uranus corresponds to the higher mind function that contains many long-term memories and strata of awareness, not just traumatic ones. Successfully mined, with attendant healing work, these memories hold gems that can unlock keys to our genius.[77]

Author/philosopher John O'Donohue alludes to this in discussing the notion of our flaws, stating that beauty (relevant, I feel, to our essence or genius) comes into a person through the "frontier" of limitation, confusion, anxiety, and helplessness (what we might call our 'flaw'), and that if we can embrace this with graciousness, we enter a doorway into another rhythm of life, one that takes us down new pathways not previously travelled.[78]

This speaks to me of the new and unknown territories that Aquarian reframing presents, when we are able to touch a fixed point of vulnerability within us, hold its fracturing of our "hope for order," and thereby open a chink or window into a new light that can shine both into and from us. This is what trauma healing entails. The 'tragic flaw,' like Uranus, and the Aquarius archetype, breaks patterns of familiarity. It is the part in us that doesn't fit, doesn't belong, doesn't meld with convention. "The world is a strange place to be," O'Donohue says, "and we are strange creatures. But strangeness needn't be frightening—it's what we see when we glimpse a wild animal, and they then quickly move away."

Wild, all-seeing mind

No surprise, then, that Aquarius is linked to wild nature, and thereby, the wildness within us, as this speaks to the part of us that has not been tamed, domesticated, colonized, or robbed of its vitality—vitality being the nature of genius and innovation. Spending time in nature, or with wild beings, or tuning into the natural rhythms of the seasons, then, helps us reconnect to our instinctual self, where our inherent essence can truly shine. And it matters, in the changing and challenging times at hand, how many of us are able to connect to our essence.

A blog post from author and theologian Matthew Fox on "The Divine Eyes" of visionary artists Alex Grey and Hildegard von Bingen[79] speaks to this. The post includes a painting of Grey's called "The Green Hand," with many eyes peering out both from within and around many green hands. The painting was created in homage to Hildegard's concept of *viriditas*

'All-seeing Mind' from the upper portion of one of my Painting Experience *works*

or "the greening" of the earth and all human work that honors it. It also speaks to the awareness that consciousness permeates all life. Fox writes,

Hildegard talks about 'the living eye,' while calling the Holy Spirit 'a fire that penetrates everything,' and God the Creator 'a brightness that shines', and Christ, the 'flashing forth that radiates divine fire.'

In my own earlier Aquarian explorations into the unknown, through the medium of *The Painting Experience*, I found myself painting multiple eyes in parts of my own paintings, indicating the witnessing presence both within and without that I instinctively felt. This valuable "process work" helped open a door to my own unique essence, or Uranian knowing.

Navigational tools for Aquarian times

Speaking of eyes, one of the gifts of Aquarius is its expansive vision, which takes in the whole, from a birds-eye, or cosmic view. Learning how to look wide, far, and deep helps us overcome our modern-day myopia and adopt a more inclusive perspective on life. This affords us some detachment from the small (albeit large-looming) dramas of our own lives.

A suggestion for learning to see with new eyes in the course of our ordinary lives is to take regular 'awe walks,' as described by UC Berkeley psychology professor, Dacher Keltner.[80] He points to the capacity for awe to help us 'get off ourselves', as was said in the days of Werner Erhard's EST trainings in the 70s. Good medicine for these over-amped Leonine selfie times. Keltner describes his research results:

We found evidence that the self can extend into the environment. In the awe-walk condition, people's selfies increasingly included less of the self. Over time, the subjects drifted off to the side, showing more of the outside environment—a street corner in San Francisco, the trees, the rocks around the Pacific Ocean. Over the course of our study, awe-walkers reported feeling less daily distress and more prosocial emotions such as compassion and amusement.

Anything that invites people back into relation with the all-that-is serves as a valuable tool for Aquarian times. And circling back to the theme of change, I came upon a recent blog post from Richard Rohr, Franciscan priest and writer, called "To Live is to Change."[81] In it he points out that being resilient means making the decision to remain open to *ongoing* (my emphasis) growth and change.

While all archetypes are of course needed, all being part of Life, Aquarius' beckoning towards taking new perspectives and adopting new stories is going to be vital to our capacity to move through the months and years ahead. We are cautioned by the wisdom of Indigenous elders, however, not to seek change or "progress" for change's sake, a trend that has led our civilization down its self-destructive path, causing us to lose respect for the time-tested rhythms and cycles of Life. We need to open to change, while also submitting to the slower, larger rhythms of life, invoking Capricorn's gift of patience.

Drawing down wisdom

Looking at the long arc of my own life, I see how my move to 'left coast' California at age 23 marked a radical departure from my traditional (read Saturnian) East Coast upbringing, perhaps indicated by my Moon's South Node (where I come from as a soul) in Aquarius, with its ruler, Uranus, conjunct my North Node (what I need to claim in this life). With Uranus co-ruling my South Node, having it conjunct my North Node reveals my soul's intent to truly embrace Uranus this time! Accordingly, it was actress Shirley Maclaine's revelatory book, *Out On a Limb*, that fired up my unique path of pursuing spiritual ideas, leading to my move to California. When I first read of the interconnectedness of all life in *The Aquarian Conspiracy* the next year, living in Berkeley, it made perfect sense to me.

Aquarius is known as a highly individualistic energy, being unafraid, and at times determined to stand apart from the crowd and follow its own path. Yet at times it is acutely aware of and concerned with its embeddedness within the whole, and thereby drawn to groups and communities that work at the levels of societal, scientific, or spiritual change and awakening.

Glass ceiling design by innovator Antonio Gaudi, Barcelona Opera House

As the last and 'farthest out' of the Air signs, Aquarius is working on consciousness development, in sharp contrast to Capricorn, whose focus is on actualizing material plane goals and ambitions. As a fixed sign, Aquarius works to deepen into its vision in anticipation of the transition to the last sign in the zodiac, Pisces, whose focus on the outer world is surrendered to the 'other'-worldly.

In tandem with Pisces, Aquarius symbolizes the greater potential within us for relating to life from a perception of Oneness, and is concerned with awakening from the chrysalis of our conditioned, separate, ego-centric perspective. Through its Uranus rulership, Aquarian energy offers us the possibility to become energetically connected or 'hooked up' to the larger reality through a consciousness that sees its true nature as part of the Whole, and is thereby inspired to contribute to the health of all life through service, whether through activism, or some form of communicating one's inner vision and wisdom, such as Thomas Merton did.

Birthing the new—Imbolc/Brigid's Day

The ancient Celts referred to the February Full Moon as the Ice Moon, and saw this month as a powerful time for sowing seeds of intention towards the year ahead. Further emphasizing this idea, the pagan cross-quarter festival of *Imbolc* (also called Brigid's Day and *Candelmas*) falls on February 2, when we are half way between winter solstice and spring equinox. This day ushers in the New Year in the pagan tradition.

At this point, we can now noticeably feel the return of the Light, and in northern California specifically, we sometimes experience unseasonably warm temperatures. So if rains have been plentiful, our brown hills are now emerald green, plum blossoms are unfurling, and lemon yellow oxalis flowers light up grassy expanses. One feels the call of 'new life,' while still under the sway of hibernation.

During the several years I spent in the early 1990s living off-grid with my husband in a tiny cabin in the remote woods and hills of western Sonoma County, I eagerly anticipated the arrival of *Imbolc*, at which point the Sun had finally climbed high enough in the sky such that it hit our single solar panel, enabling us to supplement our two propane lanterns

Lucky bee strikes early spring pay dirt in cherry blossom

with a solar panel-powered light. This marked the end of the three-month period from the prior cross-quarter, *Samhain* (Sow-win), on November 2, until now at *Imbolc*, during which the sun would have disappeared from its illuminating heights beside our little cabin beside some redwoods, impactfully darkening our cabin life.

The significance of this festival's also being named after the foremost Irish saint, Brigid of Kildare (b. 421-523), emphasizes this moment of transition as the birth of the not-yet-known. Brigid was revered as a midwife of new beginnings, and as Celtic consciousness writer/teacher John Philip Newell shares in *Sacred Earth, Sacred Soul,*[82] she was a dweller of the liminal spaces between the Divine and the human, between the womb of the Universe and what is trying to be birthed into being. She was known as well for her love of the Earth, and her modeling of female leadership.

A further link of this February festival to the fertile power of the goddess is found in the meaning of the word *Imbolc*, which is 'ewe's milk.' Given its association with birth, this festival is said to mark the 'quickening' of the year ahead, further speaking to the work of the Aquarian archetype. With the rebirth of what transpersonal astrologer Dane Rudhyar calls "the Day Force" (the Sun's light) that takes place at the winter solstice, we are now further along in sensing the light within (mirroring the course of the light without), and thus imbued with intimations of a vision for the new that will begin to manifest by spring.

Intimations of the new

Crash landing or higher ground

At a time of great flux both ecologically and politically, with social strife and polarization now the norm, it is important to create some degree of Aquarian separation from current events. Perhaps we can imagine elevating ourselves a few feet above the busy (or angry, or fear-invoking) exchange of ideas, or in some way raise ourselves to a mountaintop view of this time of rapid and dramatic change.

Aquarius certainly presides over 'alternative realities', and we do in many respects have creative choice over where we train our attention. To this end, the work of our time continues to ask that we take care with the amount of negative 'news' (much of which is tinted with spin) we imbibe, and that we keep our minds spacious and receptive, rather than ruminating excessively over losses and future fears.

Seeds of change

Top down, hierarchical rule has been the 'operating system' throughout the 2,000-year Piscean era that has preceded the Aquarian one, Pisces being the sign of 'the savior' on high. The excesses of greed and domination this system has devolved to became more acutely evident while Pluto, with its laser sharp penchant for exposure of truth, completed its journey through Capricorn—significator of corporate and other hierarchical systems. Now, with Pluto in Aquarius, and beyond that, with the longer-term Aquarian Age, we can expect a shift, with the 'messiah' concept reemerging through Unity, not a single, gifted individual or charismatic leader. But in present times, we can no longer deny the corruption of the outdated structures that have dominated us, and initially at least we are seeing a tightening of the noose—with the 'few' at the top becoming fewer, and ever richer.

Behind the scenes of 'convention', however, in keeping with the Aquarian theme of idealistic visioning, there is forward-thinking transformation work taking place across the planet in multiple realms. Some of these endeavors prioritize shadow and trauma healing work (which astrology helps access and deepen understanding of) so as to ready us with core stability and resilience for hard times ahead; others prioritize development of human and technological systems that integrate with the earth's natural intelligence. Ultimately, of course, inner healing and outer ecological and societal balancing must be woven of a piece.

The power of seeding innovative, collaborative visions of ecology-informed systemic change through the arena of learning, networking, and communication is emphasized by the transit of Uranus through Gemini until 2033, boosted by a harmonious trine with transformative Pluto. Through the end of the 2020s and into the next decade, we may feel emboldened to 'spread the world' (Gemini loves to share!) about necessary structural and habits-based changes, and ideally gather more folks to add their energy to the cause. There are many global movements being seeded online. Equally important, at the local level there are many organizations doing important work on behalf of climate change mitigation, water protection, and the building of local ecosystems resiliency.

With the 3rd House—naturally ruled by Gemini—presiding over neighbors, neighborhood groups could become seedbeds of transforming outmoded, unhealthy systems of isolation and 'going it alone', with the adoption of collaborative practices such as time banks (of which I'm an avid proponent); tool, compost and produce sharing; repair cafés; water protection; disaster preparedness; and old-fashioned neighborly connectedness.

It is important to set our compass to the 'true north' of living into a life in ways we feel good about, both within ourselves and in our daily rounds, especially as the lower octave manifestations of Aquarius—versions of Orwellian control and surveillance—continue to creep in during the initial years of Pluto's 18-year tenure in this sign. We are witnessing the dredging up of the most malign manifestations of the archetype, as this is how transformational Pluto operates, by first clearing out the dross of the sign it passes through, much like a

surgeon or shaman cleans or pulls out the diseased or broken parts inside the body in the healing process. This includes unhealthy or unjust applications of AI, as well as authoritarian rule, which we are seeing worldwide.

The off-centered or shadow aspects of Aquarius within humankind include attitudes of elitism, entrenched opinions, dependency on (or escapism through) technology and social media, exiling and othering, and fragmentation. Some may find themselves numbing out to cope with fears. But an alternative to allowing fear or rigidity (the off-balance Saturn aspects) to determine our responses is to double down on honing and living from a framework based on values of kindness, beauty, openness, inclusion, and care for all, including the earth.

Enter Deep Time

Applying ourselves to the task of living *now* as if we were already in the future we dream of suits the Aquarian perspective of the multi-dimensionality, or circularity of time. Re-membering ourselves in connection to the past, and to our ancestors, acquires new value. In what ways can we bring into the present parts of ourselves or our forebears that shone in the past? What positive, peak-moment memories can we recall from our own lives that can serve us now? Considering how time can be bent and melded, and how the natural world itself is having to adjust to off-kilter timings caused by global warming, we too might consider adjustments to our own relationship to time.

In *timely* fashion, an intriguing essay, *Wild Clocks*[83], has wafted into my inbox along the Aquarian airstrip. In it, author David Farrier discusses how 'wild clocks' in nature have fallen out of synchrony with each other, and imagines how we might likewise renew our own life rhythms.

From a deep time, 'big picture', perspective, East Indian author/researcher Bibhu Dev Misra in his recent book, *Yuga Shift*, posits that the end of the current Hindu *Kali Yuga* era of 'vice and misery' (this being the fourth, and darkest of all of the Vedic eras), arrived in March 2025. There have been much earlier, and much later dates posited for the end of this roughly 3,000-year (according to Misra) *Yuga* or 'age of the world', but in a hopeful and fascinating conversation with astrologer Daniel Giamario[84], Misra argues the mathematical premises of his prediction.

He also suggests that until 2040 we will see a period of major transformation—of simultaneous collapse and emergence—during which old structures are obliterated, and new wisdom and understanding quickens. It will take a strong act of will to break through the "assault on consciousness" that these final years of decline will present, but if we can remain open in our hearts, and conscious of our soul's work, we can make an important contribution towards the "enlightenment process" taking place beneath the surfaces, as the next Yuga promises to be built on more virtuous ground than our own. After this period, cosmic events will tilt the balance in favor of good over evil, he states. May this notion give us sustenance as we continue with our own inner healing work, and inner and outer activism.

Carl Jung, in his book, *The Undiscovered Self*, repeatedly stresses that the development of our authentic individual self is key to the positive evolution of humankind. He writes

It is, unfortunately, only too clear that if the individual is not truly regenerated in spirit, society cannot be either, for society is the sum total of individuals in need of

redemption...[the individual] is the one important factor, and the salvation of the world consists in the salvation of the individual soul.[85]

May this be a process that we are each called into, in our own ways, this creative and uplifting dance between healing and awakening the self, and serving in community, as we move forward into the unknown. May we plant and tend with care and love the seeds of new life in our own small lives, knowing we are a vital part of the larger web of the whole of life.

A RETURN TO SOURCE: PISCES

~ February 19-March 20

The Lesson of the Falling Leaves

the leaves believe
such letting go is love
such love is faith
such faith is grace
such grace is god
i agree with the leaves

- Lucille Clifton[86]

At this time on Earth, with so much that we have cherished being destroyed, dismantled or lost, the Pisces archetype calls us to the difficult work of opening to and bearing our grief, and its necessity of letting go—which Lucille Clifton so beautifully links to the falling of leaves at the end of the seasonal cycle. From its inherently transcendent perspective, Pisces also urges us to embrace the beauty and magic that the earth continues to offer in her great generosity, and to do our best to meet ourselves—and life—with compassion and faith.

Embracing that which has 'fallen,' the Pisces archetype invokes a deep and difficult work, initiating a type of dying to individual identity into a new becoming that is tuned to and guided by Source. Its ultimate prize is to meet the beauty of the Divine, and to know it—as it always has been—embedded within ourselves and the world we live in. But we must take heed to not lose our way amidst the periods of pain and confusion that this archetype presents us with, to remember, and trust, that an illumined resonance in unity with the One is ultimately on offer.

Poet Rosemerry Wahtola Trommer offers a beautiful rumination on the desire to 'unself' herself, to open into Oneness with all life, which Pisces calls us to.

> *I want to be less who I am and more what a tree is, what a star is [...],*
> *this is how I want to meet you, without a name, unencumbered by a me.*
> *I want to know myself as a collection of atoms and forces that rhyme with you,*
> *Linked as we are from the very beginning. How easy it is then to say hello,*
> *To fall in love with each other, the world.*[87]

The Piscean process invites us to abide in not knowing, to allow the unraveling of what has come before, holding onto nothing, so that we come face to face with the part of us at our core that cannot be lost. This is the part that connects us to all of life, and to spirit, in our wildness, and our nakedness. For many, facing loss, illness, or breakage head-on are necessary initiations into this other-worldly arena. But as well, Pisces/Neptune holds the keys to the realms of blissful interconnectedness that the mystics know, can we but surrender deeply enough to its mysterious ways. One of these keys is beauty, which can help quell our sorrows, and reawaken us to the presence of the hand of the Divine, if we can find the eyes to see.

As the last sign in the zodiacal wheel, Pisces, 'the fishes,' initiates us into the final release in the cycle of life. This involves a return to the generative waters from which we spring, to the all-that-is, preparing us for a time of new incarnation that arrives with the birth of spring, and the Aries archetype, signifying "I am" once again.

Saints and sinners alike

Because Pisces dwells in, or rises from the collective unconscious, those whose lives are under its sway often play roles outside the realm of the 'common things' of this world, where its polarity partner Virgo dwells. Thereby, a strong signature of Water sign Pisces can be found among spiritual seekers and mystics, nurses and caregivers, as well as prison inmates, the chronically ill, and those captured by addictions. The archetype informs those who long for something beyond the ordinary, or who feel they cannot face, or were not built to face the mundane drill of life. It is a sign of great sensitivity, which is both its gift, and its curse.

In its deep soul, Pisces knows and is often compelled by a transcendent Ideal, by that which cannot be attained or sustained here on Earth, but which is irresistible, worth even dying for. (Pisces energy can also manifest as the martyr.) However, the archetype's attunement to the ideal bears the powerful gift for creative imagining—as all things find their beginning as an idea or ideal.

In the Libra chapter I discussed the mystical relationship between the self and the Divine—between lover and beloved, as is said in Sufism—and invoked the Quranic tale of Khidr, the Green Man, who performs a type of magic before Moses at the 'place where the two seas meet'—the seas of the divine, and of the ordinary earthly realms—by bringing a dead fish back to life.

The true calling of the Pisces archetype is to learn to navigate these two seas, to be both in the world yet not of it, and to bring something 'alive' from within which issues from elsewhere, from the land of the muse, or the Creator. For Pisces truly does have one foot (sometimes its whole head!) in some aspect of the other world. Its mission is to be able to infuse its creative knowing and understanding into the collective consciousness—into Life.

Pisces' deep receptivity is enhanced by practices and pursuits that connect us with the knowing within; and its flowering emerges through such offerings as music, poetry, mystical teachings, and the arts. Musicians, filmmakers, dancers, poets, and mystical teachers alike are informed by a passion to evoke what they know and taste in the 'beyond,' or in their own depths. To do so, they regularly partake of the realms beyond time and space, from whence inspiration flows. And we as well, whether or not we consider ourselves artists or teachers, benefit from regular 'time out of time' spaces in our lives. These help us claim our full capacities for insight and inspiration.

Call to awakening

In a pivotal time of planetary transformation, life is calling for each of us to wake up from the trance of modern life—of being overtaken by our lists, our plans, and our devices. To do so, we need regular, sometimes long, infusions of Pisces. In its simplest form, we can take conscious breaks in the middle of each ordinary day, using somatic awareness and breath practices (stoplights and waiting rooms are prime opportunities).

Gentle moon beckons through gnarled oaks

Further, we can include in our days some sort of attunement to another part of our being, whether through meditation, conscious movement, music, or time outdoors, ideally in nature—imbibing the elements of air, light, water, and earth that infuse a deeper level of awareness and spaciousness into our ordinary round.

Here at the late phase of winter in Pisces time, skies are often painted varying shades of undefined grey, reflecting the Piscean lack of definition. This can be unsettling. But at times, simply tuning in to the birds' bright chatter can transport us to the realm beyond our small but focused preoccupations. Or maybe it's a sudden glimpse of "the Moon, just there at the window" (as a Rumi poem says) that reminds us of our place in a divinely given larger whole, and of our being known by this larger whole. And of course, as with all Water signs, being in the presence of water—whether its luminous sight, soothing sound, or soft touch, or even 'hydrating' ourselves well by drinking enough water, enhances our openness to the imaginal realms.

New Zealander Veda Austin, author of *The Living Language of Water,* asserts that almost all humans are dehydrated, whether literally or figuratively. She points to how in her Indigenous father's Maori language, water is referred to as "the waters," alluding to both the earth's physical waters, and the spiritual waters of life. She suggests in a podcast interview entitled, *Water as Source,*[88] that fear is inherently dehydrating. From this perspective, the modern machine is surely sapping us dry.

Waters of life in Mendocino, CA

Despite the ecological and socio-political calamities we encounter in some way almost daily, we have a choice (harkening back to the tools of the Aries Shambhala warrior) to dismantle the fear-based maya of the mind, and to replenish our psyches consistently with kindness and self-compassion. And with our connection with Earth and Sky. The alignment in the heavens now in effect (more or less until early 2027), between practical Saturn conjunct dreamy Neptune—whose imaginative powers seed our reality—sets us up perfectly to face this challenge, as it invokes the capacity to transcend fear through taking responsibility (Saturn) and harnessing faith (Neptune). Most important of all is that we take the invitation of this seminal astrological moment to tune in. As Austin says: "The secrets are in the subtleties. All the magic is in these in between realms."

Pisces is the master of subtlety, of invisibility, and of the interstitial 'in-between.'

Spaciousness and melting

Availing ourselves of the Piscean energy of unravelling, gestating, and re-forming, we are invited to create a new level of consciousness, in which we freely move between modes of 'doing' and 'being.' This means learning to integrate into our busyness and focused activity periodic shifts of rhythm so that we're not stuck in ruts or habits, or subject to tension build-up. This facilitates our capacity to flow with new thoughts and ways of doing things, as in improvisation. Surely water is forever improvising its way across the earth, en route back to the sea. When we become like water, we are more open to harvest the pure waters of spontaneous insight so needed in these uncertain, turbulent times.

Accessing the right-brained, 'illogical' mode of knowing is key to this. Brilliant British philosopher and neuroscientist Iain McGilchrist, author of *The Master and His Emissary* and, *The Matter With Things*, advocates the urgent need for a cultural shift towards a more holistic and inclusive, right-brained way of being, pointing to the disaster that the analytical, dissection-prone, left-brained culture has landed us in. To this end, on the Piscean theme, he suggests in an online talk that we consider the nail-biting phenomenon of glacial melting as not all bad, in that it exemplifies a process of release from very old and solidified ways of being.

It is certainly mind-bending to consider glacial melting in a positive light, but this is a time when all manner of new ways of looking at things is welcome. The pace of liquification of the United States government and its institutions accelerates ever more quickly as I write, not to mention the world's ecosystems. And there are many who suggest that before we can build a world worth inhabiting, the old one must go. Likewise, this dissolution process needs to take place inside ourselves. This is indeed important work, as true change on the outer always begin on the inner. This requires both courage (enter Aries), and self-compassion (Pisces/Neptune).

Taking the 'big time' perspective of glacial melt, we might again consider the astrological 'ages', which last 2100-2500 years. In a blog post about the Piscean Age from which we're emerging, and which precedes the Aquarian Age (wherein we have at least a few toes at this point, if not a whole foot), astrologer Jessica Davidson offers some valuable insights about Pisces and its work with healing, karma, and the shadow. She writes,

> As the Age of Pisces unravels, we're being challenged to actually embody the meaning of the age. That is, to embrace compassion rather than division. We must accept all parts of ourselves—including the parts we don't like—and become whole. That means resolving the split in our minds through a confrontation with the shadow—all the darkness (and light) that we've denied—to balance the opposites.
>
> Those opposites are now becoming more polarized as the shadow erupts from the depths, forcing us to deal with it. The polarization makes the opposites more visible and obvious, and undeniable. But it also reinforces our tendency to project what we've disowned onto others. That's what has to end.[89]

The ultimate fear

Let go of fear
and rest in the arms of the One
who has always held you,
the One who holds
atoms and empires
and oceans
and stars.
Let go of fear
and watch what happens next.

~ *Larry Robinson, excerpt from Rise and Fall*[90]

Sonoma, CA coast sunset

The poem excerpt above was shared in a recent public dialogue on *Life and the Meaning of Death* between the poet and a psychologist friend of mine at a local 'ideas forum'. I woke up one day shortly afterwards, ready to serve as muse for the Pisces archetype, to the shocking news that this friend had died suddenly, less than a month after the event. A remarkably fearless man himself, who had many times willingly stared death in the eye, I take my friend's sudden departure as a signal that we too must let go of fear, and "watch what happens next."

Ours is no doubt a time of dying from one way of life, into another. Facing truly radical uncertainty, here in the US and across the globe, we are wracked to varying degrees by the ultimate Piscean challenge of surrendering to undoing and unknowing, of letting go of the givens of life we have relied on and cherished. Death—endings of any sort—is our ultimate fear.

And as the last sign in the zodiacal round, Pisces is one of two archetypes that preside over such endings—the other being fellow water sign Scorpio, ruled by Pluto. But while Scorpio-Pluto's means of effecting death and transformation are prone to intensity and violence, Piscean letting go is more a gentle yielding to the tide of dissolution.

An example of the Piscean surrender process is the onset of dementia as slow gateway into the life-death transition. Memory loss for any of us can be viewed as a type of Piscean release of the mind's vigilance, something which I have been noticing quite a bit lately, both in myself and others. Faltering memory in general seems a potent sign of a time in which 'forgetting,' along with the positing of alternative truths, have become dominant strategies, and where words and concepts are lost in the blur of rapid delivery through too many channels.

The world we want to create

With Neptune's influence strengthened in the skies during its conjunction to Saturn, its 'dissolver' effect has mirrored the erosion of conditioned systems and structures. No wonder the memory waivers! The archetype is quite susceptible to both brain fog and delusion. Given that Pisces is innately a 'believer', under Neptune's sway we need to be vigilant in our media intake, practicing (Saturnian) discipline with the amount, and our sources. Even if we trust them, if the messages inject fear, and we feel that fear in our body, we can choose to redirect. This is a time to be using our minds and hearts to focus on the world we want to create, not a world of fear, violence, and destruction.

Directed positively, the Pisces archetype enhances our capacity to access and harvest gems from the imagination, in images, dreams, or metaphors that guide and inform us. And this pivotal moment in time is ripe for refining our capacity to tune in to that which lies beyond the realm of the mind, and bring it into life in some form. It is also a powerful signature for getting serious about healing work.

Relinquish victim/savior mode

One aspect of healing that Pisces/Neptune energy benefits from addressing is owning any victim roles or narratives we may still be carrying about ourselves, or any attachment to 'leading from our wounds' in certain relationships or situations. Because of Pisces' acute sensitivity, it likely *has* suffered far more deeply than less sensitive people, but carrying the victim mindset prevents us from true healing, and achieving the inner freedom, clarity, and enhanced capacity that inner healing offers.

Another shadow tendency of Pisces is that of excess self-sacrifice and service, such that it becomes built into the identity. Ultimately, those who serve to extreme can become unable to take care of their own needs, which is ultimately not a service others. The greater service is to let others face their problems on their own. This is truly tough love for Pisces!

Karmic reckoning

As referenced above, Neptunian energy conjures past karmas, bringing to the fore unresolved issues that had been locked in the unconscious. The call here, as with Scorpio, is to find the courage to be with old triggers and difficult feelings as they arise, and move through and let go of sorrows and resentments. Trauma of any sort—often ancestral—typically blocks access to our authentic heart, and thereby, our fullest creativity and self-expression. As facilitator and spiritual teacher Thomas Hubl suggests, integrated trauma from the past becomes Presence, allowing one to walk more lightly, and with a greater capacity to serve.

This may all seem rather heavy: death, memory loss, karmas rising to the fore—and it is! But these can be reframed as necessary portals of the dying, or hospice, phase of life that must be faced in order to be 'born' into a new, paradoxically stronger yet gentler, orientation to life. The systems as we've known them are going to continue to crumble, requiring that we develop new ways to flow with life's challenges and changes. In the words of writer Pico Iyer (personal friend of the Dalai Lama), "Life is about joyful participation in a world of sorrows."

Meditation practice, in whatever form, is valuable, as it nourishes us from the place inside that transcends the dramas of outer life. Also valuable is working directly with our triggers. Psychiatrist and consciousness researcher, David R. Hawkins, presents a "letting go" technique that involves taking the time to sit attentively with the discomfort in the body when a disturbance arises, and breathe attentively into the place where we feel it, without resistance, thoughts or story about the why of the trigger. The practice is of pure presence with the sensations, which typically dissipate within 5-20 minutes. True to the Piscean realms, the mind isn't needed as we meet and release difficult feelings. We can name them if we must, but the real work is in simply being present with them in their rawness, and so dissolving them.[91]

Finding our way to faith is also critical, if we are to succeed in our healing. Whatever may be our spiritual orientation, we benefit from tapping into this part of us, with the help of our open heart. Indigenous elder and teacher, Ilarion Merculieff states that true faith is based in the body's cells, and in the heart. From within the heart, one sets an intention (to serve, to heal, to trust), embodies it, and then lets go. This is how his Aleut ancestors lived, off the coast of Alaska, for centuries, having "true faith" in the transmission of 'Original Instructions' through their heart as to what to do next in order to survive over the years[92]. As Lucille Clifton says in her poem above, finding such faith is grace, and Pisces—along with ruler Neptune—is indeed the bestower of grace.

Surrender

The call to surrender that Pisces asks for is of the deepest possible *allowing,* such that our places of rigidity—our earthly forms and attitudes—are unmade, in order to be remade. This is tough, particularly when Saturn—the planetary impulse that disciplines us to rigidly hold to our material structures—is in connection with this principle, whether placed in Pisces, or in aspect to Neptune. We may feel as if trying to hold the banks of the river intact while the waters of undoing cascade wildly through them, threatening our stability.

It's hard not to see the signs that the banks are crumbling, which is why we must double down on inner work. On a recent walk in a favorite park, I noticed many fallen trees, numerous treetops broken off by winds or infestation, leaving half-size limbless trunks, with the odd woodpecker still pecking away at them. On the bike trail, I've noticed a proliferation of homeless encampments and their attendant trash. On my own street, several times in recent weeks I've picked up numerous tossed empties of Cinnamon Fireball whiskey. Drink or drugs are of course off-centered methods of coping with life out of control, but we can intentionally choose a healthier path, if so determined, and so find joy in new, hidden places.

Death/birth thresholds are heightened moments in time, and that's where we sit right now, astrologically, and in the cycle of the seasons, as well as within the larger cycle of Earth's ecological breakdown due to climate change. It's important to know that as with a birth, in the transition to death there can be a sense of celebration, and a great blessing of light. To counter the darkness that pervades any time of dying, it is our task to find and celebrate this light, wherever we may find it.

These days we face multiple systemic collapses, and many of us, the loss of loved ones as well. Our response can be to till the ground in preparation for a new consciousness, which is purified from the dross of old mindsets, delusions, and expectations, and simplified as much as possible. This impulse to purify and simplify is something Pisces shares with its polarity partner, Virgo.

Hospicing Modernity

Vanessa Andreotti, social systems academic and author of *Hospicing Modernity*, speaks beautifully to the death processes in our time. In an article, "Embracing Deep Transitions with Wisdom",[93] she writes,

> *As we stand at the precipice of endings—of species, ecosystems, organizations, and systems themselves—the work of hospicing is to move beyond fear and embrace the deep transitions ahead with wisdom. To be stewards of this time, we must develop the practices and capacities to tend to these endings, not with urgency or control, but with a kind of stillness that invites the birth of new ways of being. Endings are not failures; they are part of a cycle that requires presence, reverence, and humility.*

The qualities Andreotti invokes here speak to the Feminine ways of being, which include the capacities of listening, receptivity, stillness, and caring for life. All three Water signs move from these principals. Weaving these together with the masculine methods of action (Mars) and structuring (Saturn) helps us master the integration of opposites, which is the work of alchemical transformation.

To flow like water is to trust in Life itself, to trust that we don't need to force things to happen according to our will, or our ideas. And that we do not need to know what's next, or where we are headed. In this time of great unknowing, our strength is in our capacity to listen to and align ourselves with the subtle cues and unfoldings of life that will take us where we need to go.

When we achieve an enhanced ability for presence, attending with ease to the needs and rhythms of body and soul, of the earth, and of those with whom we commune, we can from this resourced place participate in mounting new systems sustainable for all life, and strengthening our communities. This work involves letting go of our attachments, and moving out of 'separation consciousness', as suggested at the beginning. And it involves ever bearing witness to Earth's manifestations of beauty, intelligence, and majesty.

The journey to awakening

At this critical time of death-birth midwifery on the planet, it is vital to nourish our connection to all those beings with whom we share the earth; and to the elements; the weather and the seasons; and the land, sea, and sky. We do this both through our senses, and through coaxing the mind's Silence, so that we may tap into other ways of knowing and understanding our interrelatedness with the web of life. Doing so serves as a great balm for the watery emotions brought forth by Piscean confusion, grief, and unravelling. Staying grounded in the riches of physicality warms and stirs the creative cauldron of rebirth that is not something we can know with the mind.

Dwelling in the invisible strata beyond the visible, Pisces' true work is in the not yet knowable realms from which all things spring. Finding peace, turning towards beauty, connecting through prayer and stillness, and holding to our faith are strong themes of this archetype, offering us the possibility of transcendent moments of higher knowing and being. Pisces beckons to us of the work of letting go of our small self, and opening ourselves in service to the whole. Our own inner healing and connection to the vast interconnected web of life is in effect world work, as we are all parts of the one great masterpiece of divine creation.

Astrology Primer

While by no means a comprehensive introduction to astrology, I provide this to help those less versed in astrology in their understanding of the concepts in my text, and then some!

Planets, Signs, Houses
These three concepts underlie the basic structure of astrology.

PLANETS—the "What" that is operating; core parts of the personality; actors on the celestial stage. Sometimes associated with the Greek gods.
- ✧ **Luminaries**—Sun and Moon
- ✧ **Inner or Personal Planets**—Mercury, Venus, Mars
- ✧ **Middle World or Social Planets**—Jupiter, Saturn. While considered outer planets, thes are not "transpersonal," but bridges from the personal to the societal spheres.
- ✧ **Transpersonal Planets**—Uranus, Neptune, Pluto

Planets and their Concerns
Moon—needs, feelings, security, home, mother, nourishment
- ✧ The Moon is the fastest moving celestial body, changing signs every 2.5 days.

Sun—sense of self, identity, lovability, self-worth, fuel we burn
- ✧ The Sun changes signs roughly every 30 days, and travels through the whole zodiac in a calendar year. While I've listed Sun sign dates for each archetype beneath chapter headers, they change by a day or possibly two each year, so for precision in a given year, one would need to consult an ephemeris.

Mercury—thinking, learning, connecting, communicating
Venus— relating, loving, inherent values, sense of pleasure, beauty, harmony
Mars—assertion, drive, desire, anger, sexuality, instinct

Jupiter—exploration, belief, meaning, expansion, opportunity
Saturn—limits, responsibilities, control, authority, practicality, duty

Uranus—liberation, rebellion, shock, flashes of insight, awakening

Neptune—transcendence, compassion, sacrifice, longing, service, merging

Pluto—death and transformation, regeneration, eruption, elimination, intensity

Chiron—known as "the wounded healer." Its placement indicates a sense of wounding, or inadequacy, in our persona. It shows where we have healing work to do so that we can freely offer our wisdom and healing energy to others. Ultimately our wound and our Chironic medicine are interconnected.

SIGNS—the "How" that a planet's energy operates with; flavor, or style.

Each sign is ruled by one or two planets, and carries the signature energy of that planet. By understanding the nature of a planet, you can somewhat determine the nature of the sign it rules. For example, Aries is ruled by Mars, and Aries' nature carries the qualities of the Mars archetype.

Before the three outer, transpersonal planets were discovered, the seven traditional planets and luminaries were assigned rulerships of the 12 signs. Therefore, some traditional planets rule two signs. When the transpersonal planets were discovered, they were assigned rulership of three signs—those signs thereby have both a traditional and a modern ruler. Some astrologers continue to prioritize the traditional rulers of these signs in their interpretations, while others favor the transpersonal rulers (I'm in this camp). It is important to consider both rulers.

Planetary Rulerships of the Signs

Aries—Mars

Taurus—Venus

Gemini—Mercury

Cancer—Moon

Leo—Sun

Virgo—Mercury

Libra—Venus

Scorpio—Pluto and Mars

Sagittarius—Jupiter

Capricorn—Saturn

Aquarius—Uranus and Saturn

Pisces—Neptune and Jupiter

✧ **Polarity Partners:** Signs also work as pairs, with each sign's opposite sign, or "polarity partner," sharing common themes, while also 'polar' differences. When off-centered, signs can devolve to manifesting the lowest of the opposite sign's qualities. When working at their highest level, signs integrate the best of their polarity partners.

Polarity Partner Pairs:
Aries-Libra; Taurus-Scorpio; Gemini-Sagittarius;
Cancer-Capricorn; Leo-Aquarius; Virgo-Pisces

✧ **Elements**: Signs are grouped by Elements (Earth, Air, Fire, Water) and Modalities (cardinal, fixed, mutable). Understanding elements and modalities helps us know the nature of the signs.

The Four Elements by Sign

The twelve signs are grouped into the four elements starting with Fire (Aries), and continuing in order, with Earth (Taurus), Air (Gemini), Water (Cancer), etc.

✧ Fire (Aries, Leo, Sagittarius)—magnetic, inspiring, dramatic, intuitive, instinctual, playful
✧ Earth (Taurus, Virgo, Capricorn)—practical, grounded, reliable, realistic, hard-working
✧ Air (Gemini, Libra, Aquarius)—communicative, rational, sociable, tolerant, ideas-oriented
✧ Water (Cancer, Scorpio, Pisces)—subtle, sensitive, fluid, impressionable, compassionate, private

Yin and Yang: The four elements in turn are classified as either Yin or Yang.
✧ **Yang** is associated with the Masculine principle, connoting light, action, passion, reason, and movement. Fire and Air signs are Yang.
✧ **Yin** is associated with the Feminine principle, connoting darkness, stillness, patience, intuition, and receptivity. Earth and Water signs are Yin.

Modalities

The modalities describe how energy is used; how we orient to or meet the world.

✦ Cardinal (active, dynamic, initiating)—Aries, Cancer, Libra, Capricorn

✦ Fixed (stable, tenacious, latent)—Taurus, Leo, Scorpio, Aquarius

✦ Mutable (adaptable, changeable, learning-oriented)—Gemini, Virgo, Sagittarius, Pisces

HOUSES—the "Where," or arena of life, with its specific concerns and preoccupations, in which planetary action takes place.

✦ Each of the 12 houses pertains to a sector of life relevant to the sign that naturally rules it. The "natural zodiac" has 0° Aries at the ascendant, with that point marking the beginning of the zodiacal wheel. In this way, Aries naturally rules the 1st house, and therefore the 1st house naturally pertains to the Aries/Mars enterprise; Taurus naturally rules the 2nd house realm of life, and so forth.

ASPECTS

Aspects, another tool in the astrology lexicon, describe the angular relationships between planets. These show either ease or difficulty, conflict or flow in planetary interactions.

"Hard" aspects (Conjunction, Square, Opposition) present challenges to the planets involved, and thus inspire healing work.

✦ **Conjunction** (0°) - The conjunction marks the starting point of a relational cycle involving two planets, just as the Moon's conjunction with the Sun is the start of the Sun-Moon cycle for that month. When planets are conjunct, they tend to act as one, integrating each other's energies, although if an outer planet is involved with an inner planet, it can overpower the inner planet.

✦ **Square** (90°)—Squares create internal tension or conflict between two parts of us that are at cross-purposes. It takes much inner work to come to know and reconcile these.

✦ **Opposition** (180°)—Oppositions mark the half-way point in two planet's cyclical dance. They provide perspective, and the opportunity to make adjustments in the cycle. These are typically experienced in relationship. It is common to project out one of the two planets in the opposition, and call it 'the other', but really it is also part of us.

Soft aspects (Trine and Sextile) suggest easeful partnership between planets, but do not inspire the gritty 'work' of growth transformation.

  ✧ **Trine** (120°)—Trines indicate a harmonious connection between planets, usually in the same element, that work as a team to create flow and ease.
  ✧ **Sextile** (60°)—Sextiling planets are considered as nearby helpers.

Lunar Nodes—The North and South nodes of the Moon are points in the sky where the ecliptic (the plane of the earth's orbit around the Sun) intersects the Moon's orbit around the earth. These are important in Evolutionary Astrology (a framework I use in my practice), as they indicate 'where we're coming from' in both good and outworn respects, (South) and 'where destiny is pointing us' (North).

ENDNOTES

1   I came upon the above quote when fixing myself a cup of tea, on the tea bag tag, just before starting my introduction, so I allowed it its fitting place here!

2   I, and all those astrologers whom I follow and study under, do not use astrology as a tool for prediction per se.

3   Murray Stein with Arabella Thais. "The Cosmic Codex" podcast. September 13, 2025.

4   Glenn Perry. "Towards a Postmodern Astrology," posted on his website. [I first undertook concentrated study of AstroPsychology under Perry in the mid-2000s.]

5   *The Gene Keys* is a book and an educational program by Richard Rudd, based on a system he developed as an offshoot of *Human Design*. These combine a mapping that includes astrology, the I Ching, and human DNA.

6   Jeremy Naydler. *Gardening as a Sacred Art*. Floris Books. 2011. pp. 13 & 15

7   G. Perry. "Towards a Postmodern Astrology." Perry quotes astrologer Nicholas Campion in this article.

8   Murray Stein citing C.G. Jung (quoting Michael Maier's *De circulo physico quadrotor*) in his *Collected Works, Vol. 12* . "The Human Experience of the Divine: C.G. Jung on Psychology & Spirituality" webinar for The Asheville Jung Center. December 1, 2011.

9   John Philip Newell. "John Scott and his Circle", PhD Thesis, University of Edinburgh 1981, p. 251, quoted in *Sacred Earth, Sacred Soul: Celtic Wisdom for Reawakening to What Our Souls Know and Healing the World*. Harper One, 2021. p. 145.

10   Joanna Macy's *The Work That Reconnects* can be explored online.

11   Mirabai Starr. "Lighting the Darkness." On friendsofsilence.net. January 2023.

12   Gangaji. Awakin.org (online). November 8, 2025.

13   Susan Baker Roshi. "Earth As Koan, Earth as Self". *Emergence Magazine* (online). April 1, 2024.

14   J.P. Newell. *Sacred Earth, Sacred Soul: Celtic Wisdom for Reawakening to What Our Souls Know and Healing the World*. Harper Collins, 2021. p. 6.

15   Sherri Mitchell with Vicki Robin. "What Could Possibly Go Right?" Episode 90, October 31, 2022.

16   David Hinton. *Wild Mind, Wild Earth*. Shambhala, 2022. p. 27.

17   John O'Donohue. *Beauty—The Invisible Embrace*. Harper Collins, 2004.

18   Merlin Sheldrake. Bioneers Conference. April 10, 2024.

19   David Hinton. *Wild Mind, Wild Earth*. p. 58. Shambhala. 2022.

20 " ". p. 58.

21 Leonard Cohen. published in *Beautiful Losers*. Bantam Books. 1968.

22 Vanessa Machado de Oliveira. "Smart As a Rock: Reframing Our Relationship to Intelligence". *Kosmos Journal*. Vol. 25, Issue 3.

23 Pir Zia Inayat-Khan. *The Holy Mysteries of the Five Elements*. Sufi Order International Publications, 2004. p.11.

24 Rainer Maria Rilke. Excerpt from Poem I,25, *Rilke's Book of Hours: Love Poems to God*, translated by Anita Barrows and Joanna Macy. Riverhead Books. 1995.

25 Christopher Bache. "Contemplating Reincarnation." YouTube. 2021

26 Dane Rudhyar. *The Pulse of Life*, p. 57. Shambhala. 1970.

27 Shannon Willis. "The Mycelial Art of Soft Rebellion." *Kosmos Journal*, online. Volume 25, Issue 2.

28 Mary Oliver. From "The Third Self: Mary Oliver on the Central Commitment of the Creative Life." Maria Popova, in *The Marginalian*, online.

29 Stephen Harrod Buhner. *The Secret Teachings of Plants*. p. 11. Inner Traditions International and Bear & Company, ©2004. All rights reserved. http://www.Innertraditions.com. Reprinted with permission of publisher.

30 Joseph Chilton Pearce. *The Biology of Transcendence*. Park Street Press. 2002.

31 Buhner. p. 86

32 Buhner. p. 94

33 C.J.Jung. *Mysterium Conjunctionis*. Vol 14, para 498. 1963. Quoted in *The Grail Legend*. Emma Jung & Marie-Louise von Franz. p. 191. Sigo Press. 1970

34 Arabella Thaïs. "Attunement as Governance: A New Political Possibility; The End of Hierarchy, the Dawn of Sovereignty." *Kosmos Journal*, online.

35 Safron Rossi. "The Dance of Distinctions—the Virgo Pisces Polarity." The Mercury Internet School of Psychological Astrology. 2020.

36 John O'Donohue. *Beauty: The Invisible Embrace*. Harper Perennial, 2004.

37 Llewellyn Vaughan Lee, "Where the Two Seas Meet," on goldensufi.org. October 2021.

38 A.H. Almaas, *Elements of the Real in Man*. Diamond Books, 1987. pg. 126.

39 Monica Gagliano. "The Songs of Gaia", on scienceandnonduality.com podcast. Episode 23.

40 *Vox* (online). "Why Is Putin Attacking Ukraine?" Feb. 2023.

41 Iain McGilchrist. *The Matter with Things*. Perspectiva Press. 2001

42 Liz Greene. *The Astrology of Fate*, p. 226.

43 C. G. Jung, *Answer to Job*, Bollingen Foundation. 1958.

44 Liz Greene, *The Astrology of Fate*. Red Wheel. 1984. p. 226.

45 Dane Rudhyar. *The Pulse of Life*. Shambhala, 1970. p. 78.

46 Erica Shugart. "Like Water and Wind: Resisting Massive Offshore Energy Projects in the Pacific Northwest." *Kosmos Journal.* Volume 24, Issue 5.

47 Anderson Cooper speaks with Francis Weller. "Creating A Companionship With Grief." YouTube. November 2024.

48 Liz Greene. *The Astrology of Fate*. Weiser Books. 1984. p. 41.

49 Carl Jung. *The Red Book*. W.W. Norton, 2009. A compilation of Jung's psychological observations and experiments on himself between 1913-1917.

50 Liz Greene. *The Astrological World of Jung's* Liber Novus. Routledge. 2018.

51 Michael Meade. "The Soul of Change Workshop." July 2024. Available on Mosaic Voices website.

52 Rainer Maria Rilke. *Letters To a Young Poet*, Stephen Mitchell translation. First Vintage Books. 1984. Letter 5, p. 47.

53 Richard Rudd. Genekeys.com

54 May Sarton. *Collected Poems: 1930-1933.* W.W.Norton. 1933.

55 David Hinton. *Wild Mind, Wild Earth*. Shambhala Publications, 2022. p. 113.

56 Matthew Fox. "The Mystics on Joy & Thanks (Whatever the News)." November 21, 2023.

57 Carolyn Toben. "Thomas Berry on Intuition: Recovering a Sense of the Sacred." *Kosmos Journal*. Volume 2023, Issue 3.

58 Christiana Figueres with Krista Tippett. "Ecological Hope, and Spiritual Evolution." *OnBeing*. November 9, 2023.

59 Christiana Figueres, Rebecca Solnit, Roshi Joan Halifax. Upaya Zen Center Video Series: "Uncertainty and Possibility—Meeting the Climate Future." August 11, 2023.

60 Annie Dillard. *Pilgrim at Tinker Creek*. Harper's Magazine Press. 1974.

61 Douglas Harding. *The Best Day of My Life*. Awakin.org.

62 John O'Donohue. *Beauty: The Invisible Embrace*. Sounds True Audio. Section 46, God Is Beauty.

63 Ilarion Merculieff & Shariff Abdullah. "Ancient Wisdom for Turbulent Times." November 2024. YouTube.

64 David Bohm. "Understanding Thought - Suspending Assumptions." March 2014. YouTube.

65 G.I. Gurdjieff. Quoted by J. G. Bennett. *The Masters of Wisdom*. Turnstone Books, London. 1977. p. 13.

66 Richard Rudd. *The Gene Keys: Embracing your higher purpose*. Watkins Media. 2015. p. 428.

67 Jellaludin Rumi, as quoted by Michael Meade, in an online presentation.

68 Dag Hammarskjöld. *Waymarks*. 1963.

69 Dane Rudhyar. *The Pulse of Life*, Shambhala, 1970. p.5.

70 D.H. Lawrence. *The Selected Letters of D.H. Lawrence.* ed by Diana Trilling. Farrar, Straus & Cudahy. 1958. p. 122.

71 Duane Elgin. *Choosing Earth.* Self-published. 2022.

72 Robin Wall Kimmerer. "Practical Reverence". *Emergence Magazine,* online. November 21, 2024.

73 James Hillman. Quoted in "Images of the Zodiac: Contemplating Capricorn". *Symbol Reader* blog. January 12, 2014.

74 Thomas Merton. From "Going Home to Where I Have Never Been," Presidential Address. September 22, 1959.

75 Eleanor O'Hanlon. Eyesofthewild.org.

76 "Radiation From Cellphones, Wi-Fi Is Hurting the Birds and the Bees; 5G May Make It Worse." *Newsweek.* August 27, 2018.

77 Mark Jones. *Healing the Soul: Pluto, Uranus, and the Lunar Nodes.* Raven Dreams Press. 2011.

78 John O'Donohue. *Beauty: The Invisible Embrace.* "The Beauty of the Flaw." Sounds True Audio.

79 Matthew Fox. "Alex Grey and Hildegard of Bingen on the Divine Eye(s)." DailyMeditationsWithMatthewFox.org. Jan. 2024.

80 Dacher Keltner. *Awe: The New Science of Everyday Wonder and How It Can Transform Your Life.* Excerpt quoted in "Greater Good" newsletter, UC Berkeley.

81 Richard Rohr. "To Live is to Change." *Center for Action and Contemplation* newsletter. January 1, 2024.

82 John Philip Newell. *Sacred Earth, Sacred Soul.* Harper Collins. 2021. Chapter 2.

83 David Farrier. "Wild Clocks." *Emergence Magazine.* January 23, 2025.

84 Bibu Dev Misra with Daniel Giamario. "Yuga Shift: The End of Kali Yuga." YouTube. February, 2025.

85 C.G. Jung. *The Undiscovered Self.* Berkeley. 1958. p. 56.

86 Lucille Clifton. In *How To Carry Water, Selected Poems.* BOA Editions, Ltd. 2021.

87 Rosemerry Wahtola Trommer. "It Comes Down to This." First published on AHundredFallingVeils.com. Quoted with author's permission.

88 Veda Austin. Interviewed in "For the Wild" podcast. Episode 317.

89 Jessica Davidson. "The Age of Pisces and the Transition into Aquarius." On jessicadavidson. co.uk. Quoted with author's permission.

90 Larry Robinson. Excerpt from *Rise and Fall.* Quoted with author's permission.

91 David R. Hawkins. *Letting Go: The Pathway of Surrender.* Hay House, Inc. 2012.

92 Ilarion Merculieff. From "Rites of Passage" conversation with Shariff Abdullah. Youtube (Catalylst Meditation). October 14, 2025.

93 Vanessa Andreotti. Quoted on Awakin.org, "Embracing Deep Transitions With Wisdom."

BIBLIOGRAPHY

Almaas, A.H. *Elements of the Real in Man*. Diamond Books, 1987.

Andreotti, Vanessa. "Embracing Deep Transitions with Wisdom." Awakin.org.

Bache, Christopher and Richard Rudd. *Contemplating Reincarnation*. YouTube, 2021.

Bibu Dev Misra with Daniel Giamario. "Yuga Shift: The End of Kali Yuga." YouTube, February 2025.

Bohm, David. *"Understanding Thought—Suspending Assumptions."* YouTube, March 2014.

Clifton, Lucille. *How To Carry Water: Selected Poems*. BOA Editions, Ltd., 2021.

Cohen, Leonard. *Beautiful Losers*. Bantam Books, 1968. Quoted by Safron Rossi in her webinar, "The Dance of Distinctions: Archetypal Polarities in the Zodiac: Pisces-Virgo", Mercury Internet School of Psychological Astrology.

Dillard, Annie. *Pilgrim at Tinker Creek*. Harper's Magazine Press, 1974.

Davidson, Jessica. "The Age of Pisces and the Transition into Aquarius." jessicadavidson.co.uk.

Elgin, Duane. *Choosing Earth*. Self-published, 2022.

Farrier, David. "Wild Clocks." *Emergence Magazine*, January 23, 2025.

Figueres, Christiana, with Krista Tippett. "Ecological Hope, and Spiritual Evolution." *OnBeing*, November 9, 2023.

Figueres, Christiana, Rebecca Solnit, Roshi Joan Halifax. *Upaya Zen Center Video Series: "Uncertainty and Possibility—Meeting the Climate Future."* August 11, 2023.

Fox, Matthew. "Alex Grey and Hildegard of Bingen on the Divine Eye(s)." *DailyMeditationsWithMatthewFox.org*, Jan. 2024.

Fox, Matthew. "The Mystics on Joy & Thanks (Whatever the News)." November 21, 2023.

Gagliano, Monica. "The Songs of Gaia." *Science and Nonduality* podcast, Episode 23.

Greene, Liz. *The Astrology of Fate*. Red Wheel/Weiser Books, 1984.

Greene, Liz. *The Astrological World of Jung's Liber Novus*. Routledge, 2018.

Harding, Douglas. *"The Best Day of My Life."* Awakin.org.

Hawkins, David. *Letting Go: The Pathway of Surrender*. Hay House, 2012.

Hinton, David. *Wild Mind, Wild Earth*. Shambhala, 2022.

Inayat-Khan, Pir Zia. *The Holy Mysteries of the Five Element*s. Sufi Order International Publications, 2004. p.11.

Jung, C.G. *Answer to Job*. Bollingen Foundation, 1958.

Jung, C.G. *Mysterium Conjunctionis*, Vol. 14, 1963. Quoted in *The Grail Legend*, Emma Jung & Marie-Louise von Franz, Sigo Press, 1970.

Jung, C.G. *The Red Book*. W.W. Norton, 2009.

Jung, C.G. *The Undiscovered Self*. Berkeley, 1958.

Keltner, Dacher. *Awe: The New Science of Everyday Wonder*. Excerpt in *Greater Good* newsletter, UC Berkeley.

Kimmerer, Robin Wall. "Practical Reverence." *Emergence Magazine*, online, November 21, 2024.

Lawrence, D.H. *The Selected Letters of D.H. Lawrence*, ed. Diana Trilling. Farrar, Straus & Cudahy, 1958.

Lee, Llewellyn Vaughan. "Where the Two Seas Meet." Goldensufi.org, October 2021.

Machado de Oliveira, Vanessa. "Smart As a Rock: Reframing Our Relationship to Intelligence." *Kosmos Journal*, Vol. 25, Issue 3.

Meade, Michael. "The Soul of Change Workshop." Mosaic Voices website, July 2024.

Merculieff, Ilarion & Shariff Abdullah. "Ancient Wisdom for Turbulent Times." YouTube, November 2024.

Merculieff, Ilarion. "Rites of Passage." YouTube, Catalyst Meditation, October 14, 2025.

Mitchell, Sherri, with Vicki Robin. "What Could Possibly Go Right?" podcast. Episode 90, October 31, 2022.

Merton, Thomas. "Going Home to Where I Have Never Been." Presidential Address, September 22, 1959.

Naydler, Jeremy. *Gardening as a Sacred Art*. Floris Books. 2011

Newell, John Philip. *Sacred Earth, Sacred Soul: Celtic Wisdom for Reawakening to What Our Souls Know and Healing the World*. Harper Collins, 2021.

O'Donohue, John. *Beauty: The Invisible Embrace*. Sounds True Audio, 2004.

Pearce, Joseph Chilton. *The Biology of Transcendence*. Park Street Press, 2002.

Perry, Glenn. "Towards a Postmodern Astrology." aaperry.com.

Rilke, Rainer Maria. *Rilke's Book of Hours: Love Poems to God*. Translated by Anita Barrows and Joanna Macy. Riverhead Books, 1995.

Rilke, Rainer Maria. *Letters To a Young Poet*. Stephen Mitchell translation. First Vintage Books, 1984.

Rohr, Richard. "To Live is to Change." Center for Action and Contemplation newsletter, January 1, 2024.

Rossi, Saffron. "The Dance of Distinctions—the Virgo Pisces Polarity." Mercury Internet School of Psychological Astrology, 2020.

Rudd, Richard. *The Gene Keys: Embracing Your Higher Purpose*. Watkins Media, 2015.

Rudhyar, Dane. *The Pulse of Life*. Shambhala, 1970.

Sarton, May. *Collected Poems: 1930–1933*. W.W. Norton, 1933.

Sheldrake, Merlin. Bioneers Conference, April 10, 2024.

Shugart, Erica. "Like Water and Wind: Resisting Massive Offshore Energy Projects in the Pacific Northwest." *Kosmos Journal*, Volume 24, Issue 5.

Starr, Mirabai. "Lighting the Darkness." Friendsofsilence.net, January 2023.

Toben, Carolyn. "Thomas Berry on Intuition: Recovering a Sense of the Sacred." *Kosmos Journal*, Volume 2023, Issue 3.

Trommer, Rosemerry Wahtola. Excerpt from "It Comes Down to This." AHundredFallingVeils.com.

Vox. "Why Is Putin Attacking Ukraine?" February 2023.

Willis, Shannon. "The Mycelial Art of Soft Rebellion." *Kosmos Journal*, online. Volume 25, Issue 2.

Acknowledgments

While the writing of this book was a solo endeavor, it would not have taken flight if not for the inspiration, support, and counsel of some of my precious readers, friends, and family members!

I'm grateful to friends Vicky Ness and Judith Stone, early 'adopters' of my blog missives, for each independently sowing the seed that I should turn my writings and images into an eBook. The seed germinated quietly over a long period, until my London-based brother, Dan Badger—not my most likely consumer of astrological news, but nevertheless an open-minded Gemini—persisted in taking on my potentially provocative ideas, and then watered the seed after I'd shared the book idea with him. He not only encouraged me to pursue it, but generously offered to lend me some of his publishing expertise in the process.

The next great boon came from several dear published writer friends, Tina Stanley, Sandra Lee Dennis, and Anna Gatmon, who each in different ways gave me the tools and input needed to launch the publishing of a first book. Their support and input were invaluable.

And last but very far from least, I am grateful to my beloved daughter, Alya Bohr, who miraculously found the time during her first grueling semester of graduate school to be my editor (for most of the chapters—if you find an error, it's probably one of the ones she didn't get to!) Having farmed out my own editing projects to her multiple times in the past, I knew she would be the best person for this project, and she proved me right!

Also, a big thank you to my *Earth Sky Journal* blog readers who have sent me encouraging and appreciative words over the years. While I don't write for feedback, it's encouraging to receive!

And lastly, deep gratitude to the devas of the garden, my blessed neighborhood birds, the magic of the celestial lights, and the array of wisdom teachers with whom I have had the great good fortune to apprentice myself over decades.

About the Author

Diana Badger has been a student of astrology, psychology and higher ideas, and a lover of the Earth for most of her life. Raised on the East Coast, she earned a B.A. in Comparative Literature from Brown University and began her professional life as a journalist in Washington, D.C. As her spiritual curiosity deepened, she relocated to the San Francisco Bay Area in 1985, later settling in rural Sonoma County in 1992, where she lived with her husband and raised their daughter.

For the past 20 years, Diana has woven together parallel careers as a counseling astrologer and a writer/editor, while pursuing an ongoing commitment to inner work and spiritual practice. Rooted in a reverence for the natural world and informed by multiple wisdom traditions, Diana's work reflects a lifelong inquiry into the relationship between psyche, cosmos, and Earth. She currently devotes her time to her astrology practice, her writing, and the care of home, hearth, and garden.

✧

You can contact Diana, find links to some of the resources mentioned in this book, sign up for her Earth Sky Journal, and/or peruse her astrological counseling offerings at www.dianabadger.com.

www.ingramcontent.com/pod-product-compliance
Lightning Source LLC
Chambersburg PA
CBHW041547120626
46551CB00002B/142